W9-CPC-922

5 INGREDIENTS OR LESS

COOK INSTANT

pil

Publications International, Ltd.

Pictured on the front cover: Pressure Cooker Spaghetti and Meatballs *(page 68).*

Pictured on the back cover *(top to bottom):* French Onion Soup *(page 140),* Italian Beef Sandwiches *(page 66)* and Fudgy Double Chocolate Brownies *(page 166).*

Photographs on front cover and page 37 © Shutterstock.com.

ISBN: 978-1-64558-115-4

Manufactured in China.

8 7 6 5 4 3 2 1

Note: The recipes in this book are for use in electric pressure cookers. While today's pressure cookers are built with safety features, you MUST follow the instructions which come with your pressure cooker. If you do not follow the safety instructions carefully, injury or damage may result.

Let's get social!
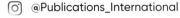 @Publications_International
@PublicationsInternational
www.pilcookbooks.com

Contents

PRESSURE COOKING BASICS

Welcome to the wonderful world of electric pressure cooking! Although the current craze makes it seem like a new invention, pressure cooking has actually been around for a few hundred years. Many people grew up hearing frightening stories of pressure cooker catastrophes—exploding pots and soup on the ceiling—but those days are long gone. There have been great changes and improvements in recent years to make modern pressure cookers completely safe, quiet and easy to use.

What exactly is a pressure cooker?

It's a simple concept: Liquid is heated in a heavy pot with a lid that locks and forms an airtight seal. Since the steam from the hot liquid is trapped inside and can't evaporate, the pressure increases and raises the boiling point of the contents in the pot, and these items cook faster at a higher temperature. In general, pressure cooking can reduce cooking time to about one third of the time used in conventional cooking methods—and typically the time spent on pressure cooking is hands off. (There's no peeking or stirring when food is being cooked under pressure.)

New and improved

Many of the electric pressure cookers on the market today are actually multi-cookers—versatile appliances that can be a pressure cooker, slow cooker, rice cooker, steamer and even a yogurt maker. The cooking programs you'll find on the different control panels are convenient shortcuts for some foods you may prepare regularly (rice, beans, stews, etc.) which use preset times and cooking levels. But you don't need any special settings to cook great food fast. In this book we'll explore the basics of pressure cooking with recipes that use customized cooking times and pressure levels. So you'll be able to cook a wide variety of delicious dishes no matter what buttons you have on your pressure cooker.

If you're accustomed to a stovetop pressure cooker, you'll need to make a few minor adjustments when using an electric one. Electric pressure cookers regulate heat automatically, so there's no worry about adjusting the heat on a burner to maintain pressure. Also, electric pressure cookers operate at less than the conventional pressure standard of 15 pounds per square inch (psi) used by stovetop pressure cookers. Most electric pressure cookers operate at 9 to 11 psi, which means that stovetop pressure cooker recipes can be adapted to electric models by adding a little more cooking time.

Pressure Cooker Components

Before beginning to cook, make sure you're familiar with the basic parts of your pressure cooker. There are some differences between brands, but they have many standard features in common. Always refer to your manual for more details and to answer questions about your specific model. (The parts are very similar but manufacturers often have different names for the same parts which can cause confusion.)

The **exterior pot** is where the electrical components are housed. It should never be immersed in water; to clean it, simply unplug the unit, wipe it with a damp cloth and dry it immediately.

The **inner pot** holds the food and fits snugly into the exterior pot. Typically made of stainless steel or aluminum with a nonstick coating, it is removable, and it can be washed by hand or some models can go in the dishwasher.

The **LED display** typically shows a time that indicates where the pressure cooker is in a particular function. For many models, the time counts down to zero from the number of minutes that were programmed. (The timing begins once the machine reaches pressure.)

The **steam release valve** (also called exhaust valve or pressure regulating valve) is on top of the lid and is used to seal the pot or release steam. To seal the pot, move the valve to the sealing or locked position; to release pressure, move the valve to the venting or open position. This valve can pop off to clean, and to make sure nothing is blocking it.

The **float valve** controls the amount of pressure inside the pressure cooker and indicates when pressure cooking is taking place—the valve rises once the contents of the pot reach working pressure; it drops down when all the pressure has been released after cooking.

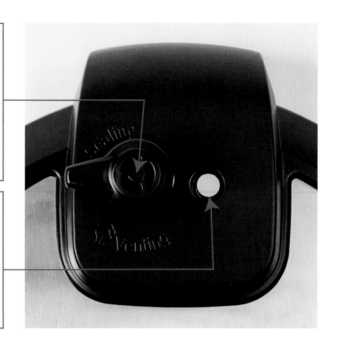

The **anti-block shield** or case is a small stainless steel cage found on the inside of the lid that prevents the pressure cooker from clogging. It can be removed for cleaning.

The **silicone sealing ring** (also called a gasket) underneath the lid helps create a tight seal to facilitate pressure cooking. The sealing ring has a tendency to absorb strong odors from cooking (particularly from acidic ingredients); washing it regularly with warm soapy water (or in the dishwasher if allowed) will help these odors dissipate, as will storing your pressure cooker with the lid ring side up. If you cook both sweet and savory dishes frequently, you may want to purchase an extra sealing ring (so the scent of curry or pot roast doesn't affect your rice pudding or crème brûlée). Make sure to inspect the ring before cooking—if it has any splits or cracks, it will not work properly and should be replaced.

Pressure Cooking for Beginners

Every recipe is slightly different, but most include these basic steps. Read through the entire recipe before beginning to cook so you'll know what ingredients to add and when to add them, which pressure level to use, the cooking time and the release method.

1. Sauté or brown: Many recipes call for sautéing vegetables or browning meat at the beginning of a recipe to add flavor. (Be sure to leave the lid off in this step.)

2. Add the ingredients as the recipe directs and secure the lid, making sure it is properly locked according to the instruction manual. Turn the pressure release valve to the sealing or locked position.

3. Choose the pressure level and set the cooking time. (The default setting is usually high pressure, which is what most recipes use.) Depending on your model, the pressure cooker may start automatically or you may need to press the Start button.

4. Once the pressure cooking is complete, use the pressure release method directed by the recipe. There are three types of releases:

Natural release: Let the pressure slowly release on its own, which can take anywhere from 5 to 25 minutes (but is typically in the 10- to 15-minute range). The release time will be shorter for a pot that is less full and longer for one that is more full. When the float valve lowers, the pressure is released and you can open the lid.

Quick release: Use a towel or pot holder to manually turn the pressure release valve to the venting or open position immediately after the cooking is complete. Be sure to get out of the way of the steam, and position the pressure cooker on your countertop so the steam doesn't get expelled straight into your cabinets (or in your face). It can take up to 2 minutes to fully release all the pressure.

A combination of natural and quick release: The recipe will instruct you to let the pressure release naturally for a certain amount of time (frequently for 10 minutes), and then do a quick release as directed.

Rules of Release

Releasing pressure can be a little confusing when you first start using your pressure cooker. There's no need to worry at all about safety—you won't be able to open the lid until all the pressure has been released. And you don't need to guess which release to use since the recipes will tell you. But there are some important things to know about releasing pressure, especially when you start cooking and experimenting with the pressure cooker on your own.

Natural release is best for meats (especially larger roasts and tough cuts), foods that generate a lot of foam, such as grains, dried beans and legumes, and foods that are primarily liquid, such as soups.

Quick release is best for foods with shorter cooking times, such as vegetables and eggs, and more delicate ingredients like fish and chicken breasts. It is also used when adding additional ingredients to the pot, as is the case with some stews and vegetable dishes, and to check whether a food is done.

A **combination release** is best when a full natural release is too slow but a quick release might cause food or foam to spray through the pressure release valve.

The release method does affect the cooking time—food continues to cook during a natural release due to the residual pressure and steam in the pot. So you may discover in some dishes that you prefer a shorter cooking time with a longer release time or vice versa. (Unfortunately the two times are not in direct proportion, so it can take some trial and error to figure out what works best.)

The In's and Out's of Pressure Cooking

Getting a cake pan, bowl or ceramic dish in and out of the pressure cooker may seem tricky but simply requires the right tools. Some wire racks come with handles that support your pan and help move it into and out of the pot, but if you don't have one, it's easy to make a foil sling using 12- to 18-inch-wide heavy-duty aluminum foil . Tear off a piece of foil 30 inches long, then fold the piece lengthwise three times to make a long strip about 4 to 6 inches wide. Lay the strip on the countertop and place the pan in the center of the strip. Pull the ends up around the side of the pan to lift it into and out of the pressure cooker. Fold down the ends of the sling before putting the lid on the pressure cooker. After cooking, dry off the foil sling; it can be re-used many times.

The 5-Ingredient Pantry

The key to creating quick, easy and delicious dishes with five ingredients is having a well-stocked pantry. When you always have the basics on hand (see below), you might only need a few items at the grocery store—you can skip the long lines and have dinner on your table (or in your pressure cooker) in no time!

> **The recipes in this book can all be created with five ingredients and/or the addition of these common pantry items:**
>
> - **WATER**
> - **BROTH**
> - **BUTTER**
> - **VEGETABLE OIL**
> - **OLIVE OIL**
> - **ALL-PURPOSE FLOUR**
> - **CORNSTARCH**
> - **GRANULATED SUGAR**
> - **BROWN SUGAR**
>
> - **COMMON DRIED HERBS AND SPICES** (such as ground cinnamon, ground nutmeg, ground red pepper, red pepper flakes, garlic powder, dried oregano, dried thyme, paprika, etc.).
>
> Keep a few time-saving spice blends on hand too, such as Italian seasoning, chili powder, Southwestern seasoning, pumpkin pie spice, etc.

These pantry items and any optional ingredients are listed in the recipes in black type, while the rest of the ingredients are listed in red type. So it's always easy to know just what you need with a quick glance. You'll find that when you put your pantry and your pressure cooker to work, you can create fabulous meals any time of day with less effort and less time—it's pressure cooking made simple.

BREAKFAST & BRUNCH

Sticky Cinnamon Monkey Bread
MAKES 6 TO 8 SERVINGS

⅓ cup sugar

1 tablespoon ground cinnamon

1 container (about 16 ounces) refrigerated jumbo biscuits (8 biscuits)

¼ cup (½ stick) butter, melted

1 cup water

1. Spray 6-cup bundt pan with nonstick cooking spray. Combine sugar and cinnamon in medium bowl; mix well. Sprinkle 1 tablespoon cinnamon-sugar in bottom of prepared pan.

2. Separate biscuits; cut each biscuit into quarters. Dip each biscuit piece in butter; roll in cinnamon-sugar to coat. Layer biscuit pieces in prepared pan. Cover pan with foil.

3. Pour water into pot. Place rack in pot; place pan on rack using foil sling (see page 8) or handles of rack.

4. Secure lid and move pressure release valve to sealing or locked position. Cook at high pressure 25 minutes.

5. When cooking is complete, use natural release for 10 minutes, then release remaining pressure. Uncover; let stand 10 minutes. Invert monkey bread onto plate; serve warm.

Fruity Whole Grain Cereal

MAKES 4 TO 6 SERVINGS

2¼ **cups water**

¼ cup steel-cut oats

¼ cup uncooked pearl barley

¼ cup uncooked brown rice

½ **teaspoon salt**

½ cup milk

¾ cup chopped dried fruit blend

2 **tablespoons packed brown sugar**

½ **teaspoon ground cinnamon**

1. Combine water, oats, barley, rice and salt in pot; mix well.

2. Secure lid and move pressure release valve to sealing position. Cook at high pressure 20 minutes.

3. When cooking is complete, use natural release for 10 minutes, then release remaining pressure.

4. Stir in milk, dried fruit, brown sugar and cinnamon; mix well. Serve hot. Refrigerate any leftover cereal in airtight container.

> **TIP:** To reheat cereal, place one serving in microwavable bowl. Microwave on HIGH 30 seconds; stir. Add water or milk to reach desired consistency. Microwave just until hot.

French Toast Casserole

MAKES 6 SERVINGS

1 loaf (14 to 16 ounces)
   day-old cinnamon
   swirl bread
   (see Tip)

4 ounces cream
   cheese, cubed

1½ cups whole milk

4 eggs

¼ cup maple syrup,
   plus additional
   for serving

⅛ teaspoon salt

1 cup water

1. Spray 1½-quart (6- to 7-inch) soufflé dish with nonstick cooking spray. Cut bread into 1-inch pieces. (You should have 5 to 6 cups bread cubes.) Place one third of bread in prepared dish; top with half of cream cheese cubes. Repeat layers; top with remaining bread.

2. Whisk milk, eggs, ¼ cup maple syrup and salt in medium bowl until well blended. Pour over bread and cream cheese; press gently into liquid. Cover with foil; let stand 30 minutes.

3. Pour water into pot. Place rack in pot; place soufflé dish on rack using foil sling (see page 8) or handles of rack.

4. Secure lid and move pressure release valve to sealing or locked position. Cook at high pressure 35 minutes.

5. When cooking is complete, use natural release for 5 minutes, then release remaining pressure. Uncover; let stand 5 minutes before serving. Cut into wedges; serve warm with additional maple syrup.

> **TIP:** Day-old bread is drier than fresh bread and better able to absorb the custard mixture in casseroles and bread puddings. If you only have fresh bread, bake the bread cubes on a baking sheet in a preheated 350°F oven about 7 minutes or until lightly toasted.

Lemon Blueberry Oatmeal

MAKES 4 SERVINGS

2 tablespoons butter

1¼ cups steel-cut oats

3¾ cups water

½ teaspoon salt

2 lemons

4 tablespoons honey, divided

¾ cup fresh blueberries

½ cup chopped toasted almonds*

To toast almonds, cook in small skillet over medium heat about 5 minutes or until lightly browned and fragrant, stirring frequently.

1. Press Sauté; melt butter in pot. Add oats, cook about 6 minutes or until oats are lightly browned and fragrant, stirring frequently. Stir in water and salt; mix well.

2. Secure lid and move pressure release valve to sealing or locked position. Cook at high pressure 12 minutes.

3. Grate 4 teaspoons peel from lemons; squeeze 3 tablespoons juice.

4. When cooking is complete, use natural release for 10 minutes, then release remaining pressure. Stir oats until smooth. Add lemon juice, 2 teaspoons grated peel and 2 tablespoons honey; mix well.

5. Top each serving with blueberries, almonds and remaining lemon peel; drizzle with remaining honey.

Kale and Roasted Pepper Frittata

MAKES 6 SERVINGS

10 eggs

½ cup whole milk

1 **teaspoon Greek seasoning**

2 cups baby kale*

1 cup (4 ounces) crumbled feta cheese with sun-dried tomatoes and basil

¾ cup diced roasted red peppers

1½ **cups water**

Or substitute 2 cups baby arugula or baby spinach.

1. Spray 1½-quart (6- to 7-inch) soufflé dish with nonstick cooking spray. Beat eggs, milk and Greek seasoning in medium bowl until well blended. Stir in kale, feta and roasted peppers. Pour into prepared dish; cover with foil.

2. Pour water into pot. Place rack in pot; place soufflé dish on rack using foil sling (see page 8) or handles of rack.

3. Secure lid and move pressure release valve to sealing or locked position. Cook at high pressure 30 minutes.

4. When cooking is complete, use natural release for 10 minutes, then release remaining pressure. Uncover; let stand 5 minutes before serving.

Pancake Breakfast Casserole

MAKES 6 SERVINGS

4 eggs

1 cup half-and-half

2 tablespoons sugar

¾ teaspoon ground cinnamon, plus additional for garnish

½ teaspoon vanilla

9 frozen buttermilk pancakes (4-inch diameter), cut in half

1 cup water

Maple syrup

1. Spray 1½-quart (6- to 7-inch) soufflé dish with nonstick cooking spray. Whisk eggs, half-and-half, sugar, ¾ teaspoon cinnamon and vanilla in medium bowl until well blended.

2. Arrange 4 or 5 pancake halves standing up around side of prepared dish. Stack remaining pancake halves in soufflé dish, making layers as even as possible. Pour egg mixture over pancakes; press pancakes gently into liquid. Cover with foil; refrigerate overnight.

3. Remove soufflé dish from refrigerator at least 30 minutes before cooking. Pour water into pot. Place rack in pot; place soufflé dish on rack using foil sling (see page 8) or handles of rack.

4. Secure lid and move pressure release valve to sealing or locked position. Cook at high pressure 30 minutes.

5. When cooking is complete, use natural release for 5 minutes, then release remaining pressure. Uncover; let stand 5 minutes before serving. Sprinkle with additional cinnamon, if desired. Cut into wedges; serve warm with maple syrup.

Apple Pie Breakfast Risotto

MAKES 6 SERVINGS

4 tablespoons (½ stick) butter, divided

4 medium Granny Smith apples (about 1½ pounds), peeled and diced

1½ teaspoons apple pie spice, divided

1½ cups uncooked arborio rice

1 teaspoon salt

4 cups apple juice

2 tablespoons packed brown sugar, plus additional for serving

Optional toppings: milk, sliced almonds and/or dried cranberries

1. Press Sauté; melt 2 tablespoons butter in pot. Add apples and ½ teaspoon apple pie spice; cook and stir about 5 minutes or until apples are softened. Transfer to small bowl; set aside.

2. Melt remaining 2 tablespoons butter in pot. Add rice, remaining 1 teaspoon apple pie spice and salt; cook and stir 1 minute. Stir in apple juice and 2 tablespoons brown sugar; mix well.

3. Secure lid and move pressure release valve to sealing or locked position. Cook at high pressure 6 minutes.

4. When cooking is complete, press Cancel and use quick release. Press Sauté; add reserved apples to pot. Cook and stir 1 minute or until risotto reaches desired consistency. Serve with additional brown sugar and desired toppings.

Crustless Spinach Quiche

MAKES 6 SERVINGS

6 eggs

¾ cup half-and-half

¾ **teaspoon Italian seasoning**

½ **teaspoon salt**

½ **teaspoon black pepper**

1 package (10 ounces) frozen chopped spinach, thawed and squeezed dry

1 cup (4 ounces) shredded Italian cheese blend

1½ **cups water**

1. Spray 7-inch metal cake pan with nonstick cooking spray. Beat eggs, half-and-half, Italian seasoning, salt and pepper in medium bowl until well blended. Stir in spinach and cheese; mix well. Pour into prepared pan; cover with foil.

2. Pour water into pot. Place rack in pot; place pan on rack using foil sling (see page 8) or handles of rack.

3. Secure lid and move pressure release valve to sealing or locked position. Cook at high pressure 28 minutes.

4. When cooking is complete, use natural release for 5 minutes, then release remaining pressure. Uncover; let stand 5 minutes before serving.

TIP: To remove the quiche from the pan, run a knife around the edge of the pan to loosen. Invert the quiche onto a plate; invert again onto a second plate. Cut into wedges.

Classic Irish Oatmeal

MAKES 4 SERVINGS

2 tablespoons butter

1 cup steel-cut oats

3 cups water

½ teaspoon salt

½ teaspoon ground cinnamon

Berry Compote (optional, recipe follows)

⅓ cup half-and-half

¼ cup packed brown sugar

1. Press Sauté; melt butter in pot. Add oats; cook about 6 minutes or until oats are lightly browned and fragrant, stirring frequently. Add water, salt and cinnamon; cook and stir 1 minute.

2. Secure lid and move pressure release valve to sealing or locked position. Cook at high pressure 13 minutes. Meanwhile, prepare Berry Compote, if desired.

3. When cooking is complete, press Cancel to turn off heat. Use natural release for 10 minutes, then release remaining pressure.

4. Stir oats until smooth. Add half-and-half and brown sugar; stir until well blended. If thicker oatmeal is desired, press Sauté and cook 2 to 3 minutes or until desired thickness, stirring constantly. (Porridge will also thicken upon standing.) Serve with Berry Compote, if desired.

Berry Compote:

Combine 1 cup quartered fresh strawberries, 6 ounces fresh blackberries, 6 ounces fresh blueberries, 3 tablespoons granulated sugar and 1 tablespoon water in medium saucepan; bring to a simmer over medium heat. Cook 8 to 9 minutes or until berries are tender but still hold their shape, stirring occasionally.

Parmesan Garlic Monkey Bread

MAKES 6 TO 8 SERVINGS

2 tablespoons butter, melted

2 tablespoons olive oil

2 cloves garlic, minced

1 teaspoon Italian seasoning

¼ teaspoon salt

1 cup grated Parmesan cheese (do not use shredded)

1 container (about 16 ounces) refrigerated jumbo biscuits (8 biscuits)

1 cup water

1. Spray 6-cup bundt pan with nonstick cooking spray. Combine butter, oil, garlic, Italian seasoning and salt in medium bowl; mix well. Place cheese in shallow dish.

2. Separate biscuits; cut each biscuit into quarters. Dip each biscuit piece in butter mixture; roll in cheese to coat. Layer biscuit pieces in prepared pan. Cover pan with foil.

3. Pour water into pot. Place rack in pot; place pan on rack using foil sling (see page 8) or handles of rack.

4. Secure lid and move pressure release valve to sealing or locked position. Cook at high pressure 25 minutes. Preheat oven to 400°F. Line small baking sheet with foil; spray with cooking spray.

5. When cooking is complete, use natural release for 10 minutes, then release remaining pressure. Uncover; let stand 10 minutes. Invert monkey bread onto prepared baking sheet. Bake about 10 minutes or until top is golden brown.

POULTRY

Chicken Enchilada Chili
MAKES 4 SERVINGS

1 can (about 14 ounces) diced tomatoes with green chiles, drained

1 can (10 ounces) red enchilada sauce

½ **teaspoon salt**

¼ **teaspoon ground cumin**

⅛ **teaspoon black pepper**

1½ pounds boneless skinless chicken thighs, cut into 1-inch pieces

1 cup frozen or canned corn

2 tablespoons finely chopped fresh cilantro

Optional toppings: shredded pepper jack cheese, sliced green onions

1. Combine tomatoes, enchilada sauce, salt, cumin and pepper in pot; mix well. Add chicken; stir to coat.

2. Secure lid and move pressure release valve to sealing or locked position. Cook at high pressure 5 minutes.

3. When cooking is complete, use natural release for 10 minutes, then release remaining pressure.

4. Press Sauté; add corn to pot. Cook about 6 minutes or until chili is reduced and thickens slightly, stirring frequently. Stir in cilantro. Serve with desired toppings.

Hoisin Barbecue Chicken Sliders

MAKES 16 SLIDERS

⅔ cup hoisin sauce

⅓ cup barbecue sauce

1 tablespoon soy sauce

¼ **teaspoon red pepper flakes**

3 to 3½ pounds boneless skinless chicken thighs

2 **tablespoons water**

1 **tablespoon cornstarch**

16 dinner rolls or Hawaiian sweet rolls, split

1. Combine hoisin sauce, barbecue sauce, soy sauce and red pepper flakes in pot; mix well. Add chicken; stir to coat.

2. Secure lid and move pressure release valve to sealing or locked position. Cook at high pressure 8 minutes.

3. When cooking is complete, use natural release for 5 minutes, then release remaining pressure. Remove chicken to plate; let stand until cool enough to handle. Shred chicken into bite-size pieces.

4. Stir water into cornstarch in small bowl until smooth. Press Sauté; add cornstarch mixture to pot. Cook and stir about 2 minutes or until sauce thickens.

5. Return chicken to pot; mix well. Spoon about ¼ cup chicken onto each roll.

One-Pot Chinese Chicken Soup

MAKES 4 SERVINGS

1 container **(32 ounces) chicken broth**

⅓ cup reduced-sodium soy sauce

1 pound boneless skinless chicken thighs

1 package (16 ounces) frozen stir-fry vegetable blend (do not thaw)

6 ounces uncooked dried thin Chinese egg noodles

1 to 3 tablespoons sriracha sauce

1. Combine broth and soy sauce in pot; mix well. Add chicken. Secure lid and move pressure release valve to sealing or locked position. Cook at high pressure 8 minutes.

2. When cooking is complete, press Cancel and use quick release. Remove chicken to bowl; set aside 5 minutes or until cool enough to handle. Shred chicken into bite-size pieces.

3. Press Sauté; add vegetables and noodles to broth mixture in pot. Cook about 3 minutes or until noodles are tender. Stir in chicken and 1 tablespoon sriracha sauce; taste and add additional sauce for a spicier flavor.

Buffalo Chicken Wings

MAKES 4 TO 6 SERVINGS

3 pounds chicken wings, tips discarded, separated at joints

1 teaspoon garlic powder

1 teaspoon salt, divided

½ cup water

⅔ cup hot pepper sauce

⅓ cup butter, melted

1½ teaspoons Worcestershire sauce

1 teaspoon packed brown sugar

1. Season wings with garlic powder and ¾ teaspoon salt. Pour water into pot. Place rack in pot; place wings on rack (or use steamer basket to hold wings).

2. Secure lid and move pressure release valve to sealing or locked position. Cook at high pressure 5 minutes.

3. Meanwhile, preheat broiler. Line baking sheet with foil. Combine hot pepper sauce, butter, Worcestershire sauce, brown sugar and remaining ¼ teaspoon salt in large bowl; mix well.

4. When cooking is complete, press Cancel and use quick release. Pat wings dry with paper towels; add to bowl of sauce and toss well to coat. Spread wings in single layer on prepared baking sheet. (Reserve sauce left in bowl.)

5. Broil about 6 minutes or until browned. Turn and brush with sauce; broil 4 to 5 minutes or until browned. Return wings to bowl with sauce; toss to coat.

Pressure Cooker Rotisserie Chicken

MAKES 4 SERVINGS

1 whole chicken
(about 4 pounds)

2 tablespoons
rotisserie chicken
seasoning
(see Tip)

1 tablespoon butter

1 tablespoon olive oil

1 cup chicken broth

Fresh parsley sprigs
and lemon wedges
(optional)

1. Pat chicken dry. Tie drumsticks together with kitchen string and tuck wing tips under. Sprinkle seasoning inside cavity and over all sides of chicken, pressing to adhere.

2. Press Sauté; heat butter and oil in pot. Add chicken, breast side up; cook about 5 minutes or until browned. Turn chicken over using tongs and spatula; cook about 5 minutes or until browned. Remove chicken to plate.

3. Add broth to pot; cook 1 minute, scraping up browned bits from bottom of pot. Place rack in pot; place chicken on rack, breast side up.

4. Secure lid and move pressure release valve to sealing or locked position. Cook at high pressure 21 minutes.

5. When cooking is complete, use natural release for 15 minutes, then release remaining pressure. Remove chicken to cutting board; tent with foil and let stand 10 minutes before carving. If desired, strain cooking liquid and serve with chicken. Garnish, if desired.

Note:

When fully cooked, the temperature of the chicken (tested in the thigh) should be 165°F. A chicken larger than 4 pounds may take an additional 3 minutes to cook, while a smaller chicken may take a few minutes less.

TIP: Rotisserie chicken seasoning is available in the spice section of many supermarkets. If you can't find it, there are other simple seasoning options for this recipe. Use a basic poultry seasoning or Italian seasoning and add 1 teaspoon of salt and 1 teaspoon of paprika. Or use your favorite seasoning blend.

Chipotle BBQ Turkey Sandwiches

MAKES 4 SERVINGS

1 tablespoon
vegetable oil

1 small red onion,
chopped

½ teaspoon chipotle
chili powder

¾ cup plus
2 tablespoons
barbecue sauce,
divided

1 package (24 ounces)
turkey tenderloins
(2 tenderloins),
each cut in half

4 sandwich buns

1. Press Sauté; heat oil in pot. Add onion; cook and stir 3 minutes or until softened. Add chipotle chili powder; cook and stir 30 seconds. Stir in ¾ cup barbecue sauce; mix well. Add turkey; turn to coat.

2. Secure lid and move pressure release valve to sealing or locked position. Cook at high pressure 20 minutes.

3. When cooking is complete, use natural release for 10 minutes, then release remaining pressure. Remove turkey to bowl; let stand 5 minutes or until cool enough to handle. Shred into bite-size pieces.

4. Meanwhile, press Sauté; adjust heat to low. Cook sauce in pot 5 minutes or until slightly reduced.

5. Add shredded turkey and remaining 2 tablespoons barbecue sauce to pot; cook 2 minutes, stirring frequently. Serve on buns.

Tuesday Night Tacos

MAKES 4 SERVINGS

1 tablespoon vegetable oil

1½ pounds boneless skinless chicken thighs

1 cup chunky salsa

Corn tortillas, warmed

½ cup shredded lettuce

1 cup pico de gallo

1 cup (4 ounces) shredded Cheddar cheese (optional)

1. Press Sauté; heat oil in pot. Add chicken; cook 4 to 5 minutes or until browned on both sides. Add salsa; cook 1 minute, scraping up browned bits from bottom of pot. Turn chicken to coat with salsa.

2. Secure lid and move pressure release valve to sealing or locked position. Cook at high pressure 11 minutes.

3. When cooking is complete, press Cancel and use quick release. Use two forks or tongs to shred chicken into bite-size pieces in pot.

3. Serve chicken mixture in tortillas with lettuce, pico de gallo and cheese, if desired.

Pressure Cooker Chicken Adobo

MAKES 4 SERVINGS

⅓ cup cider vinegar

⅓ cup reduced-sodium
　soy sauce

5 cloves garlic, minced

3 bay leaves

1 **teaspoon black
　pepper**

2½ pounds bone-in
　skin-on chicken
　thighs (about 6)

　**Hot cooked rice
　(optional)**

　**Sliced green onion
　(optional)**

1. Combine vinegar, soy sauce, garlic, bay leaves and pepper in pot; mix well. Add chicken; turn to coat. Arrange chicken skin side down in liquid.

2. Secure lid and move pressure release valve to sealing or locked position. Cook at high pressure 13 minutes. Preheat broiler. Line baking sheet with foil.

3. When cooking is complete, use natural release for 10 minutes, then release remaining pressure. Remove chicken to prepared baking sheet, skin side up.

4. Broil about 4 minutes or until skin is browned and crisp. Meanwhile, press Sauté; cook liquid in pot about 5 minutes or until slightly reduced. Serve sauce over chicken and rice, if desired. Garnish with green onion.

Salsa Verde Chicken Stew

MAKES 4 TO 6 SERVINGS

2 cans (about 15 ounces each) black beans, rinsed and drained

1½ pounds boneless skinless chicken breasts, cut into 1-inch pieces

1 jar (16 ounces) salsa verde

1½ cups frozen corn

¾ cup chopped fresh cilantro

Diced avocado and tortilla chips (optional)

1. Combine beans, chicken and salsa in pot; mix well.

2. Secure lid and move pressure release valve to sealing or locked position. Cook at high pressure 4 minutes.

3. When cooking is complete, press Cancel and use quick release. Press Sauté; add corn to pot. Cook about 3 minutes or until heated through. Stir in cilantro; mix well. Serve with avocado and tortilla chips, if desired.

Mustard Garlic Turkey Breast

MAKES 4 TO 6 SERVINGS

1 tablespoon
   vegetable oil

1 boneless turkey
   breast (about
   3½ pounds),
   skin removed

2 tablespoons spicy
   brown mustard

2 tablespoons
   chopped fresh
   parsley

1 clove garlic, minced

1 teaspoon salt

½ teaspoon black
   pepper

1½ cups water

¼ cup all-purpose flour
   (optional)

1. Press Sauté; heat oil in pot. Add turkey; cook about 10 minutes or until browned on all sides.

2. Meanwhile, combine mustard, parsley, garlic, salt and pepper in small bowl; mix well. Remove turkey from pot; rub herb mixture over turkey. Pour water into pot. Place rack in pot; place turkey on rack.

3. Secure lid and move pressure release valve to sealing or locked position. Cook at high pressure 30 minutes.

4. When cooking is complete, use natural release for 10 minutes, then release remaining pressure. Remove turkey to cutting board; tent with foil. Let stand 10 minutes before slicing.

5. If desired, prepare gravy with cooking liquid. Stir ½ cup cooking liquid into flour in small bowl until smooth. Press Sauté; add flour mixture to pot. Cook 5 minutes or until gravy thickens, stirring frequently.

Asian Chicken and Noodles

MAKES 4 SERVINGS

1 tablespoon
  vegetable oil

1 pound boneless
  skinless chicken
  breasts, cut into
  1×½-inch pieces

1 bottle or jar (about
  12 ounces) stir-fry
  sauce

¾ **cup chicken broth
  or water**

8 ounces uncooked
  thin Pad Thai rice
  noodles (⅛ inch
  wide)

1 package (16 ounces)
  frozen stir-fry
  vegetable blend
  (do not thaw)

1. Press Sauté; heat oil in pot. Add chicken; cook about 4 minutes or until no longer pink, stirring frequently.

2. Stir in sauce and broth; mix well. Top with noodles, breaking to fit as necessary. Cover with vegetables in even layer. (Do not stir.)

3. Secure lid and move pressure release valve to sealing or locked position. Cook at high pressure 2 minutes.

4. When cooking is complete, press Cancel and use quick release. Stir with tongs to separate noodles and coat noodles and vegetables with sauce. If there is excess liquid in pot, press Sauté; cook and stir 2 minutes or until liquid has evaporated.

Classic Deviled Eggs

MAKES 6 SERVINGS

1 **cup water**

6 eggs

  Ice water

3 tablespoons
   mayonnaise

1 tablespoon minced
   fresh dill *or*
   1 teaspoon
   dried dill weed

1 teaspoon Dijon
   mustard

¼ **teaspoon salt**

⅛ **teaspoon white**
   pepper

  Paprika (optional)

1. Pour 1 cup water into pot. Place rack in pot; place eggs on rack (or use steamer basket to hold eggs).

2. Secure lid and move pressure release valve to sealing or locked position. Cook at low pressure 9 minutes.

3. When cooking is complete, press Cancel and use quick release. Immediately remove eggs to bowl of ice water; let cool 5 to 10 minutes.

4. Peel eggs; cut in half lengthwise. Transfer yolks to small bowl. Add mayonnaise, minced dill, mustard, salt and pepper; mash with fork until well blended.

5. Fill egg halves with yolk mixture using teaspoon or piping bag fitted with large plain tip. Garnish with paprika.

TIP: You can use this method to cook 3 to 12 eggs. If you don't need to use the eggs right away, store them unpeeled in the refrigerator for up to 1 week. For soft-boiled eggs, cook at low pressure 3 to 4 minutes. For eggs in between soft and hard-cooked, cook at low pressure 5 to 7 minutes. Remove to a bowl of ice water after cooking as directed above.

BEEF

Barbecue Beef Sandwiches
MAKES 4 SERVINGS

2½ pounds boneless beef chuck roast, cut in half

2 tablespoons Southwest seasoning

1 tablespoon vegetable oil

½ cup beef broth

1½ cups barbecue sauce, divided

4 sandwich or pretzel buns, split

1⅓ cups prepared coleslaw* (preferably vinegar based)

Prepared coleslaw can be found in the deli department at most supermarkets. Vinegar-based coleslaws provide a perfect complement to the rich beef; they can often be found at the salad bar or prepared foods section of large supermarkets.

1. Sprinkle both sides of beef with Southwest seasoning. Press Sauté; heat oil in pot. Add beef; cook about 6 minutes per side or until browned. Remove to plate.

2. Add broth to pot; cook 2 minutes, scraping up browned bits from bottom of pot. Stir in ½ cup barbecue sauce. Return beef to pot; turn to coat.

3. Secure lid and move pressure release valve to sealing or locked position. Cook at high pressure 60 minutes.

4. When cooking is complete, use natural release for 15 minutes, then release remaining pressure. Remove beef to large bowl; let stand until cool enough to handle. Shred beef into bite-size pieces. Stir in remaining 1 cup barbecue sauce.

5. Fill buns with beef mixture; top with coleslaw.

Pressure Cooker Meat Loaf

MAKES 6 SERVINGS

1 tablespoon olive oil

1 small onion, finely chopped

½ red bell pepper, finely chopped

1 teaspoon garlic powder

1 teaspoon dried oregano

1½ cups water

2 pounds ground meat loaf mix *or* 1 pound each ground beef and ground pork

1 egg

3 tablespoons tomato paste

1 teaspoon salt

½ teaspoon black pepper

1. Press Sauté; heat oil in pot. Add onion, bell pepper, garlic powder and oregano; cook and stir 3 minutes or until vegetables are softened. Remove to large bowl; let cool 5 minutes. Wipe out pot with paper towels; add water and rack to pot.

2. Add meat loaf mix, egg, tomato paste, salt and black pepper to vegetable mixture; mix well. Tear off 18×12-inch piece of foil; fold in half crosswise to create 12×9-inch rectangle. Shape meat mixture into 7×5-inch oval on foil; bring up sides of foil to create pan, leaving top of meat loaf uncovered. Place foil with meat loaf on rack in pot.

3. Secure lid and move pressure release valve to sealing or locked position. Cook at high pressure 37 minutes.

4. When cooking is complete, press Cancel and use quick release. Remove meat loaf to cutting board; tent with foil. Let stand 10 minutes before slicing.

Italian Short Ribs

MAKES 4 SERVINGS

2 tablespoons vegetable oil

3 pounds bone-in beef short ribs, trimmed and cut into 3-inch pieces

1 teaspoon Italian seasoning

¾ teaspoon salt

¼ teaspoon black pepper

1½ cups chopped leeks (2 to 3 leeks)

½ cup dry white wine

¾ cup pitted kalamata or oil-cured olives

1¼ cups prepared pasta sauce

Hot cooked polenta or mashed potatoes (optional)

1. Press Sauté; heat oil in pot. Add short ribs in batches; cook about 8 minutes or until browned on all sides. Remove to plate; season with Italian seasoning, salt and pepper. Drain off all but 1 tablespoon fat.

2. Add leeks to pot; cook and stir 2 minutes or until softened. Add wine; cook until almost evaporated, scraping up browned bits from bottom of pot. Return short ribs to pot with olives; pour pasta sauce over short ribs.

3. Secure lid and move pressure release valve to sealing or locked position. Cook at high pressure 30 minutes.

4. When cooking is complete, use natural release for 10 minutes, then release remaining pressure. Serve short ribs and sauce with polenta, if desired.

Speedy Meatball Subs

MAKES 6 SERVINGS

1 jar (24 ounces) pasta sauce

1 pound frozen Italian-style meatballs

6 sub or hoagie rolls, split and toasted

12 slices provolone cheese

Chopped fresh parsley (optional)

1. Pour half of pasta sauce into pot. Place meatballs in single layer in sauce; top with remaining sauce.

2. Secure lid and move pressure release valve to sealing or locked position. Cook at high pressure 11 minutes. Preheat oven to 400°F. Line baking sheet with foil.

3. When cooking is complete, press Cancel and use quick release. Place rolls on prepared baking sheet. Bake 3 minutes or until lightly toasted.

4. Spoon sauce and meatballs on bottom halves of rolls; top with cheese slices (two per sandwich). Bake about 3 minutes or until cheese melts. Sprinkle with parsley, if desired; top with top halves of rolls.

Corned Beef and Cabbage

MAKES 3 TO 4 SERVINGS

1 corned beef brisket
(3 to 4 pounds)
with seasoning
packet

2 cups water

1 head cabbage
(1½ pounds), cut
into 6 wedges

1 package (16 ounces)
baby carrots

1. Place corned beef in pot, fat side up; sprinkle with seasoning. Pour water into pot.

2. Secure lid and move pressure release valve to sealing or locked position. Cook at high pressure 90 minutes.

3. When cooking is complete, use natural release for 10 minutes, then release remaining pressure. Remove beef to cutting board; tent with foil.

4. Add cabbage and carrots to pot. Secure lid and move pressure release valve to sealing or locked position. Cook at high pressure 4 minutes. When cooking is complete, press Cancel and use quick release.

5. Slice corned beef; serve with vegetables.

Tex-Mex Chili

MAKES 4 TO 6 SERVINGS

4 slices bacon, chopped

⅓ cup all-purpose flour

1 teaspoon salt, divided

¼ teaspoon black pepper

2 pounds boneless beef top round or chuck shoulder steak, cut into ½-inch pieces

1 medium onion, chopped, plus additional for garnish

2 cloves garlic, minced

1¼ cups water

1 package (1¼ ounces) Tex-Mex chili seasoning mix

1. Press Sauté; cook bacon in pot until crisp. Remove to paper towel-lined plate.

2. Combine flour, ½ teaspoon salt and black pepper in large resealable food storage bag. Add beef; toss to coat. Add beef to bacon drippings in two batches; cook about 5 minutes or until browned. Remove to plate.

3. Add onion to pot; cook and stir 3 minutes or until softened. Add garlic; cook and stir 1 minute. Return beef and bacon to pot. Add water, chili seasoning mix and remaining ½ teaspoon salt; cook and stir 2 minutes, scraping up browned bits from bottom of pot.

4. Secure lid and move pressure release valve to sealing or locked position. Cook at high pressure 20 minutes.

5. When cooking is complete, use natural release for 10 minutes, then release remaining pressure. Serve with additional onion, if desired.

> **TIP:** Texas chili doesn't contain any beans. But if you want to stretch this recipe and dilute some of the spiciness—and you don't live in Texas!—you can add canned pinto beans to the chili after the pressure has been released. Press Sauté and cook until the beans are heated through.

Italian Beef Sandwiches

MAKES 4 SERVINGS

1 jar (16 ounces) sliced
  pepperoncini

1 jar (16 ounces)
  giardiniera

2 to 2½ pounds
  boneless beef
  chuck roast

½ **cup beef broth**

1 **tablespoon Italian
  seasoning**

4 French or sub rolls,
  split

1. Drain pepperoncini, reserving ½ cup liquid. Set aside ½ cup pepperoncini for sandwiches. Drain giardiniera, reserving ½ cup vegetables for sandwiches.

2. Combine beef, remaining pepperoncini, reserved ½ cup pepperoncini liquid, remaining giardiniera vegetables, broth and Italian seasoning in pot.

3. Secure lid and move pressure release valve to sealing or locked position. Cook at high pressure 60 minutes.

4. When cooking is complete, use natural release for 15 minutes, then release remaining pressure. Remove beef to large bowl; let stand until cool enough to handle. Shred into bite-size pieces. Add ½ cup cooking liquid; toss to coat.

5. Fill rolls with beef, reserved pepperoncini and reserved giardiniera vegetables. Serve with warm cooking liquid for dipping.

Pressure Cooker Spaghetti and Meatballs

MAKES 6 SERVINGS

1 pound frozen meatballs

8 ounces uncooked spaghetti, broken in half

1 tablespoon olive oil

¾ teaspoon salt

2 cups water

1 jar (24 ounces) chunky marinara sauce

Grated Parmesan cheese and fresh basil leaves (optional)

1. Place meatballs in pot in single layer. Arrange pasta in criss-crossing layers over meatballs; drizzle with oil.

2. Stir salt into water in measuring cup. Pour pasta sauce and water over pasta, making sure to cover pasta completely.

3. Secure lid and move pressure release valve to sealing or locked position. Cook at high pressure 9 minutes.

4. When cooking is complete, press Cancel and use quick release. Gently stir to separate pasta and blend with sauce. Garnish, if desired.

Southwestern Chile Beef

MAKES 4 SERVINGS

2 tablespoons vegetable oil

2 pounds beef round roast, cut into 1-inch pieces

1 onion, finely chopped

2 cloves garlic, minced

1 teaspoon all-purpose flour

1 teaspoon salt

1 teaspoon dried oregano

½ teaspoon ground cumin

¼ teaspoon black pepper

5 canned whole green chiles, chopped

1 canned chipotle pepper in adobo sauce, chopped

Hot cooked polenta, rice or pasta (optional)

1. Press Sauté; heat 1 tablespoon oil in pot. Add half of beef; cook about 5 minutes or until browned, stirring occasionally. Remove to plate. Add remaining oil and beef; cook 3 minutes, stirring occasionally. Add onion and garlic; cook and stir 3 minutes or until beef is browned and onion is softened.

2. Return first half of beef to pot. Add flour, salt, oregano, cumin and black pepper; cook and stir 30 seconds. Stir in green chiles and chipotle pepper; mix well.

3. Secure lid and move pressure release valve to sealing or locked position. Cook at high pressure 35 minutes.

4. When cooking is complete, use natural release for 5 minutes, then release remaining pressure.

5. Press Sauté; cook 5 to 10 minutes or until sauce is reduced and thickens slightly. Serve with polenta, if desired.

Quick French Dip

MAKES 6 SERVINGS

3 pounds boneless beef chuck roast

½ **teaspoon salt**

½ **teaspoon black pepper**

1 **tablespoon olive oil**

2 onions, cut into halves, then cut into ¼-inch slices

⅔ **cup reduced-sodium beef broth**

3 tablespoons Worcestershire sauce

6 hoagie rolls, split

12 slices provolone cheese

1. Season beef with salt and pepper. Press Sauté; heat oil in pot. Add beef; cook about 6 minutes per side or until well browned. Remove to cutting board.

2. Add onions to pot; cook 6 to 8 minutes or until golden brown, stirring occasionally. Remove half of onions to small bowl; set aside. Stir in broth and Worcestershire sauce; mix well. Cut beef into 3-inch pieces; return to pot and turn to coat.

3. Secure lid and move pressure release valve to sealing or locked position. Cook at high pressure 45 minutes.

4. When cooking is complete, use natural release for 15 minutes, then release remaining pressure. Remove beef to large bowl; let stand until cool enough to handle. Shred into bite-size pieces. Add ⅔ cup cooking liquid; toss to coat. Strain remaining cooking liquid for serving, if desired.

5. Top bottom halves of rolls with cheese, beef and reserved onions. Serve sandwiches with warm au jus for dipping.

Brisket with Vegetables

MAKES 8 SERVINGS

1 tablespoon
    vegetable oil

1 beef brisket
    (4 to 5 pounds),
    trimmed

2 onions, thinly sliced

4 cloves garlic, minced

2 teaspoons dried
    thyme

1 cup beef broth

1 teaspoon salt

½ teaspoon black
    pepper

2 pounds unpeeled
    red potatoes,
    quartered

1 pound baby carrots

3 tablespoons water

2 tablespoons
    all-purpose flour

1. Press Sauté; heat oil in pot. Add brisket; cook until browned on all sides. Remove to plate. Add onions to pot; cook and stir 3 minutes or until softened. Add garlic, and thyme; cook and stir 1 minute. Add broth, salt and pepper; cook and stir 1 minute, scraping up browned bits from bottom of pot. Return brisket to pot.

2. Secure lid and move pressure release valve to sealing or locked position. Cook at high pressure 60 minutes.

3. When cooking is complete, use natural release for 10 minutes, then release remaining pressure.

4. Add potatoes and carrots to pot. Secure lid and move pressure release valve to sealing or locked position. Cook at high pressure 10 minutes. When cooking is complete, use natural release for 10 minutes, then release remaining pressure. Remove brisket and vegetables to platter; tent with foil.

5. Stir water into flour in small bowl until smooth. Add ¼ cup hot cooking liquid; stir until blended. Press Sauté; add flour mixture to remaining cooking liquid in pot. Cook and stir 3 to 4 minutes or until sauce thickens.

6. Slice brisket across the grain. Serve brisket and vegetables with sauce.

Italian Beef Ragu

MAKES 6 SERVINGS

2 pounds boneless beef chuck roast, cut into 2-inch pieces

½ **teaspoon salt**

½ **teaspoon black pepper**

1 **tablespoon olive oil**

1 onion, chopped

½ **cup plus 2 tablespoons beef broth, divided**

1 jar (24 ounces) garlic and herb pasta sauce

¼ cup plus 1 tablespoon red wine vinegar, divided

Hot cooked pappardelle pasta

1. Season beef with salt and pepper. Press Sauté; heat oil in pot. Add beef in two batches; cook about 5 minutes or until browned. Remove to plate. Add onion and 2 tablespoons broth; cook and stir 3 minutes or until softened, scraping up browned bits from bottom of pot.

2. Reserve ¾ cup pasta sauce; set aside. Add remaining pasta sauce, ½ cup broth and ¼ cup vinegar to pot; mix well. Return beef and accumulated juices to pot; stir to coat.

3. Secure lid and move pressure release valve to sealing or locked position. Cook at high pressure 45 minutes.

4. When cooking is complete, use natural release for 15 minutes, then release remaining pressure. Remove beef to large bowl; let stand 5 minutes or until cool enough to handle.

5. Meanwhile, press Sauté; adjust heat to low. Add reserved ¾ cup pasta sauce and remaining 1 tablespoon vinegar to pot; cook 5 minutes, stirring occasionally.

6. Shred beef; stir into sauce. Taste and season with additional salt and pepper, if desired. Serve over pasta.

PORK

Tacos with Carnitas
MAKES 6 SERVINGS

2 tablespoons chili powder

1 tablespoon salt

1 tablespoon dried oregano

1 teaspoon ground cumin

1 medium onion, quartered

2 bay leaves

2 pounds pork leg, shoulder or roast, trimmed, cut into 4 pieces

1½ cups water

Corn tortillas, warmed

Optional toppings: shredded lettuce, salsa, crumbled Cotija cheese

1. Combine chili powder, salt, oregano and cumin in small bowl; mix well. Place onion and bay leaves in pot. Place pork on top of onion; sprinkle with spice mixture. Pour water into pot.

2. Secure lid and move pressure release valve to sealing or locked position. Cook at high pressure 75 minutes.

3. When cooking is complete, use natural release for 10 minutes, then release remaining pressure. Remove pork from liquid with tongs; place in 13×9-inch baking pan or on baking sheet lined with foil. Preheat broiler.

4. Remove onion and bay leaves from cooking liquid. Press Sauté; cook 10 minutes or until liquid is slightly reduced. Meanwhile, separate pork into large shreds with tongs; spread out in baking pan. Broil about 3 minutes or until browned.

5. Pull pork into smaller shreds with tongs or two forks. Place pork in medium bowl; add 1 cup cooking liquid and toss to coat. Add additional liquid, if desired. Serve pork in tortillas with desired toppings.

Maple Spice Rubbed Ribs

MAKES 4 SERVINGS

3 teaspoons chili powder, divided

1¼ teaspoons garlic powder, divided

¾ teaspoon salt

½ teaspoon black pepper

3 to 3½ pounds pork baby back ribs, trimmed and cut into 4-rib sections

4 tablespoons maple syrup, divided

1 can (8 ounces) tomato sauce

½ teaspoon pumpkin pie spice

1. Combine 1½ teaspoons chili powder, ¾ teaspoon garlic powder, salt and pepper in small bowl; mix well. Brush ribs with 2 tablespoons maple syrup; rub with spice mixture. Place ribs in pot.

2. Combine tomato sauce, remaining 2 tablespoons maple syrup, 1½ teaspoons chili powder, ½ teaspoon garlic powder, and pumpkin pie spice in medium bowl; mix well. Pour over ribs in pot; stir to coat ribs with sauce.

3. Secure lid and move pressure release valve to sealing or locked position. Cook at high pressure 25 minutes.

4. When cooking is complete, use natural release for 10 minutes, then release remaining pressure. Remove ribs to plate; tent with foil.

5. Press Sauté; cook about 10 minutes or until sauce thickens. Brush ribs with sauce; serve remaining sauce on the side.

Hot and Sweet Sausage Sandwiches

MAKES 5 SERVINGS

1½ cups pasta sauce

1 large sweet onion, cut into ¼-inch slices

2 medium bell peppers (green, red or one of each), cut into ½-inch slices

1½ tablespoons packed brown sugar

1 package (16 ounces) hot Italian sausage links (5 sausages)

5 Italian rolls, split

1. Combine pasta sauce, onion, bell peppers and brown sugar in pot; mix well. Add sausages to pot; spoon some of sauce mixture over sausages.

2. Secure lid and move pressure release valve to sealing or locked position. Cook at high pressure 5 minutes.

3. When cooking is complete, use natural release for 10 minutes, then release remaining pressure. Remove sausages to plate; tent with foil.

4. Press Sauté; cook 10 minutes or until sauce is reduced by one third, stirring occasionally. Serve sausages in rolls; top with sauce.

TIP: If you have leftover sauce, refrigerate or freeze it and serve over pasta or polenta. Top with grated Parmesan cheese.

Pork Loin with Apples and Onions

MAKES 4 SERVINGS

2 tablespoons vegetable oil

1 bone-in or boneless pork loin roast (about 3 pounds), trimmed

2 medium onions, chopped

2 sweet-tart apples such as Braeburn, Honeycrisp or Jonagold, peeled and thinly sliced

¾ cup lager beer

2 tablespoons packed brown sugar

1 teaspoon ground ginger

½ teaspoon salt

½ teaspoon ground cinnamon

½ teaspoon black pepper

⅛ teaspoon ground red pepper

1. Press Sauté; heat oil in pot. Add pork; cook about 8 minutes or until browned on all sides. Remove to plate.

2. Add onions to pot; cook and stir 6 minutes or until lightly browned. Add apples, beer, brown sugar, ginger, salt, cinnamon, black pepper and red pepper; cook and stir 1 minute, scraping up browned bits from bottom of pot. Return pork to pot.

3. Secure lid and move pressure release valve to sealing or locked position. Cook at high pressure 35 minutes.

4. When cooking is complete, use natural release for 10 minutes, then release remaining pressure. Remove pork to cutting board; tent with foil.

5. Press Sauté; cook about 10 minutes or until sauce is reduced by one third, stirring occasionally. Serve with pork.

> **TIP:** Pork should be cooked to an internal temperature of at least 145°F. Use an instant-read thermometer to check the temperature of the pork after releasing the pressure. If necessary, cook an additional few minutes.

Chili Verde

MAKES 4 SERVINGS

1 tablespoon
    vegetable oil

1 pound boneless
    pork loin, cut
    into 1-inch pieces

1 onion, halved and
    thinly sliced

1 pound tomatillos,
    husks removed,
    rinsed and
    coarsely chopped

1 **teaspoon garlic**
    powder

1 **teaspoon ground**
    cumin

1 can (about
    15 ounces) Great
    Northern beans,
    rinsed and drained

1 can (4 ounces) diced
    green chiles

1 **teaspoon salt**

¼ **teaspoon black**
    pepper

   Chopped fresh
    cilantro (optional)

1. Press Sauté; heat oil in pot. Add pork; cook about 6 minutes or until browned, stirring occasionally. Remove to plate.

2. Add onion to pot; cook and stir 3 minutes or until softened. Add tomatillos, garlic powder and cumin; cook and stir 3 minutes, scraping up browned bits from bottom of pot. Stir in beans, chiles, salt, pepper and pork; mix well.

3. Secure lid and move pressure release valve to sealing or locked position. Cook at high pressure 8 minutes.

4. When cooking is complete, use natural release for 10 minutes, then release remaining pressure. Sprinkle with cilantro, if desired.

Pulled Pork Sandwiches

MAKES 6 TO 8 SERVINGS

2 tablespoons coarse salt

2 tablespoons packed brown sugar

2 tablespoons paprika

1 teaspoon dry mustard

1 teaspoon black pepper

3 pounds boneless pork shoulder roast, cut into 3-inch pieces

1 cup ketchup

⅓ cup cider vinegar

6 to 8 large sandwich rolls or buns, split

¾ cup barbecue sauce

1. Preheat oven to 325°F. Combine salt, brown sugar, paprika, mustard and pepper in small bowl; mix well. Rub mixture all over pork.

2. Combine ketchup and vinegar in pot; mix well. Place pork pieces in sauce; do not stir.

3. Secure lid and move pressure release valve to sealing or locked position. Cook at high pressure 60 minutes.

4. When cooking is complete, use natural release for 10 minutes, then release remaining pressure. Remove pork to medium bowl. Reserve ½ cup cooking liquid from pot.

5. Shred pork into bite-size pieces when cool enough to handle. Toss with reserved cooking liquid, if desired. Serve warm on rolls with barbecue sauce.

Ale'd Pork and Sauerkraut

MAKES 4 TO 6 SERVINGS

2 teaspoons paprika

1 teaspoon garlic powder

½ teaspoon salt

¼ teaspoon black pepper

3½ pounds boneless pork shoulder or pork butt roast, trimmed

1½ tablespoons vegetable oil

1 jar (32 ounces) sauerkraut, drained

1 cup ale or dark beer

1 tablespoon sugar

1. Combine paprika, garlic powder, salt and pepper in small bowl; mix well. Rub mixture all over pork.

2. Press Sauté; heat oil in pot. Add pork; cook about 8 minutes or until browned on all sides. Remove to plate.

3. Add sauerkraut, ale and sugar to pot; cook and stir 2 minutes, scraping up browned bits from bottom of pot. Return pork to pot, pressing into sauerkraut mixture.

4. Secure lid and move pressure release valve to sealing or locked position. Cook at high pressure 45 minutes.

5. When cooking is complete, use natural release for 10 minutes, then release remaining pressure. Remove pork to cutting board; tent with foil. Let stand 10 minutes before slicing. Serve with sauerkraut and cooking liquid remaining in pot.

Perfect BBQ Ribs

MAKES 4 SERVINGS

1 rack pork baby back ribs (about 3 pounds)

⅓ **cup barbecue seasoning or grilling rub**

2 cups apple juice

¼ cup cider vinegar

1 tablespoon liquid smoke

1 cup barbecue sauce, plus additional for serving

1. Remove membrane covering bones on underside of ribs. Rub barbecue seasoning generously over both sides of ribs, pressing to adhere.

2. Combine apple juice, vinegar and liquid smoke in pot; mix well. Stand ribs vertically in liquid with meaty side facing out, coiling ribs into a ring to fit in pot.

3. Secure lid and move pressure release valve to sealing or locked position. Cook at high pressure 20 minutes. Preheat broiler. Line baking sheet with foil.

4. When cooking is complete, use natural release for 5 minutes, then release remaining pressure. Remove ribs to prepared baking sheet, meaty side up. Brush both sides of ribs with barbecue sauce.

5. Broil about 5 minutes or until sauce begins to bubble and char. Cut into individual ribs; serve with additional sauce.

Cider Pork and Onions

MAKES 8 SERVINGS

1 tablespoon
   vegetable oil

4 pounds bone-in
   pork shoulder
   roast*

4 onions, cut into
   ¼-inch slices
   (about 4 cups)

1 cup apple cider,
   divided

1 **teaspoon salt,
   divided**

4 cloves garlic, minced

1 **teaspoon dried
   rosemary**

½ **teaspoon black
   pepper**

*A 4-pound roast requires an
8-quart pressure cooker to fit.*

1. Press Sauté; heat oil in pot. Add pork; cook until browned on all sides. Remove to plate. Add onions, ¼ cup cider and ½ teaspoon salt to pot; cook 8 minutes or until onions are softened, scraping up browned bits from bottom of pot. Add garlic and rosemary, cook and stir 1 minute. Return pork to pot; sprinkle with remaining ½ teaspoon salt and pepper. Pour remaining ¾ cup cider over pork.

2. Secure lid and move pressure release valve to sealing or locked position. Cook at high pressure 75 minutes.

3. When cooking is complete, use natural release. Remove pork to cutting board; tent with foil.

4. Meanwhile, press Sauté; cook 10 to 15 minutes or until sauce is reduced by one third. Skim fat from sauce; season with additional salt and pepper. Cut pork; serve with sauce.

GRAINS & BEANS

Classic Macaroni and Cheese
MAKES 4 TO 6 SERVINGS

2 cups uncooked elbow macaroni

2 cups water

1½ **teaspoons salt, divided**

1 can (5 ounces) evaporated milk

3 cups (12 ounces) shredded Colby-Jack cheese*

⅛ **teaspoon black pepper**

*Or substitute 6 ounces each shredded Colby and Monterey Jack cheeses.

1. Combine macaroni, water and 1 teaspoon salt in pot. Secure lid and move pressure release valve to sealing or locked position. Cook at high pressure 4 minutes.

2. When cooking is complete, press Cancel and use quick release.

3. Press Sauté; alternately add evaporated milk and handfuls of cheese, stirring constantly until cheese is melted and smooth. Stir in remaining ½ teaspoon salt and pepper.

Winter Squash Risotto

MAKES 4 TO 6 SERVINGS

2 tablespoons butter

1 tablespoon olive oil

1 large shallot or small onion, finely chopped

1½ cups uncooked arborio rice

4 cups vegetable or chicken broth

2 cups cubed butternut squash (½-inch pieces)

1 teaspoon salt

½ teaspoon dried thyme

¼ teaspoon black pepper

½ cup grated Parmesan or Romano cheese, plus additional for garnish

1. Press Sauté; heat butter and oil in pot. Add shallot; cook and stir 2 minutes or until softened. Add rice; cook and stir 4 minutes or until rice is translucent. Stir in broth, squash, salt, thyme and pepper; mix well.

2. Secure lid and move pressure release valve to sealing or locked position. Cook at high pressure 6 minutes.

3. When cooking is complete, press Cancel and use quick release.

4. Press Sauté; adjust heat to low. Cook risotto about 3 minutes or until desired consistency, stirring constantly. Stir in ½ cup cheese. Serve immediately with additional cheese.

Jalapeño Cheddar Cornbread

MAKES 8 SERVINGS

1 cup yellow cornmeal

¾ **cup all-purpose flour**

¼ **cup sugar**

2 **teaspoons baking powder**

1 **teaspoon salt**

1 buttermilk or whole milk

2 eggs

3 **tablespoons butter, melted**

1 cup (4 ounces) shredded Cheddar cheese

2 jalapeño peppers, seeded and minced

1½ **cups water**

1. Spray 7-inch springform pan with nonstick cooking spray. Combine cornmeal, flour, sugar, baking powder and salt in large bowl; mix well.

2. Whisk buttermilk, eggs and butter in medium bowl until blended. Add to cornmeal mixture; stir just until blended. Stir in cheese and jalapeños until blended. Spread batter evenly in prepared pan; smooth top. Cover pan with foil.

3. Pour water into pot. Place rack in pot; place pan on rack using foil sling (see page 8) or handles of rack.

4. Secure lid and move pressure release valve to sealing or locked position. Cook at high pressure 30 minutes.

5. When cooking is complete, press Cancel and use quick release. Uncover; cool on wire rack 5 minutes before serving.

Easy Dirty Rice

MAKES 4 TO 6 SERVINGS

1½ cups uncooked long grain rice

8 ounces bulk Italian sausage

1½ **cups water**

1 onion, finely chopped

1 green bell pepper, finely chopped

½ cup finely chopped celery

1½ **teaspoons salt**

¼ **teaspoon black pepper**

¼ **teaspoon ground red pepper**

Chopped fresh parsley (optional)

1. Rinse rice well; drain in fine-mesh strainer.

2. Press Sauté; cook sausage in pot 6 to 8 minutes or until browned, stirring to break up meat. Drain fat. Stir in rice, water, onion, bell pepper, celery, salt, black pepper and red pepper; mix well.

3. Secure lid and move pressure release valve to sealing or locked position. Cook at high pressure 4 minutes.

4. When cooking is complete, use natural release for 10 minutes, then release remaining pressure. Fluff rice with fork. Sprinkle with parsley, if desired.

Shortcut Baked Beans

MAKES 6 TO 8 SERVINGS

5 slices thick-cut bacon, chopped

1 small onion, chopped

3½ **cups water**

1 pound dried pinto beans, rinsed and sorted

1 cup barbecue sauce

¼ cup ketchup

½ **teaspoon salt**

1. Press Sauté; cook bacon in pot until crisp. Drain off all but 1 tablespoon drippings.

2. Add onion to pot; cook and stir 3 minutes or until softened. Add water and beans; cook and stir 1 minute, scraping up browned bits from bottom of pot. Stir in barbecue sauce and ketchup; mix well.

3. Secure lid and move pressure release valve to sealing or locked position. Cook at high pressure 50 minutes.

4. When cooking is complete, use natural release for 15 minutes, then release remaining pressure. Stir beans; season with ½ teaspoon salt. If there is excess liquid in pot, press Sauté and cook 3 to 5 minutes or until liquid is reduced, stirring frequently.

Asparagus-Parmesan Risotto

MAKES 4 TO 6 SERVINGS

4 tablespoons (½ stick) butter, divided

1 tablespoon olive oil

1 onion, finely chopped

1½ cups uncooked arborio rice

4 cups vegetable broth

1 teaspoon salt

2½ cups fresh asparagus pieces (about 1 inch)

⅔ cup frozen peas

1 cup grated Parmesan cheese, plus additional for serving

1. Press Sauté; heat 3 tablespoons butter and oil in pot. Add onion; cook and stir 2 minutes or until softened. Add rice; cook and stir 2 minutes or until rice is translucent. Add broth and salt; mix well.

2. Secure lid and move pressure release valve to sealing or locked position. Cook at high pressure 5 minutes.

3. When cooking is complete, press Cancel and use quick release.

4. Stir in asparagus and peas. Secure lid and move pressure release valve to sealing or locked position. Cook at high pressure 1 minute.

5. When cooking is complete, press Cancel and use quick release. Stir in remaining 1 tablespoon butter and 1 cup cheese. Garnish with additional cheese.

Asparagus-Spinach Risotto:

Substitute 1 cup baby spinach or chopped fresh spinach leaves for peas. Proceed as directed.

Penne with Ricotta, Tomatoes and Basil

MAKES 4 SERVINGS

2 cans (about 14 ounces each) diced tomatoes with basil, garlic and oregano

2½ cups water

3 teaspoons salt, divided

1 package (16 ounces) uncooked penne pasta

1 container (15 ounces) ricotta cheese

⅔ cup chopped fresh basil

¼ cup olive oil

1 tablespoon balsamic vinegar

¼ teaspoon black pepper

Grated Parmesan cheese (optional)

1. Combine tomatoes, water and 2 teaspoons salt in pot; mix well. Stir in pasta.

2. Secure lid and move pressure release valve to sealing or locked position. Cook at high pressure 5 minutes.

3. Meanwhile, combine ricotta, basil, oil, vinegar, remaining 1 teaspoon salt and pepper in medium bowl; mix well.

4. When cooking is complete, press Cancel and use quick release. Drain any remaining liquid in pot.

5. Add ricotta mixture to pot; stir gently to coat. Sprinkle with Parmesan, if desired.

Cheesy Polenta

MAKES 6 SERVINGS

5 cups vegetable broth

½ teaspoon salt

1½ cups uncooked instant polenta

½ cup grated Parmesan cheese

¼ cup (½ stick) butter, cubed, plus additional for serving

Fried sage leaves (optional)

1. Combine broth and salt in pot; slowly whisk in polenta until blended.

2. Secure lid and move pressure release valve to sealing or locked position. Cook at high pressure 5 minutes.

3. When cooking is complete, use natural release for 5 minutes, then release remaining pressure.

4. Whisk in cheese and ¼ cup butter until well blended. (Polenta may appear separated immediately after cooking but will come together when stirred.) Serve with additional butter; garnish with sage.

Note:

Chicken broth may be substituted for vegetable broth. Or use water and add an additional ½ teaspoon salt when whisking in the polenta.

TIP: Spread any leftover polenta in a baking dish and refrigerate until cold. Cut the cold polenta into sticks or slices, brush with olive oil and pan-fry or grill until lightly browned.

Pesto Rice and Beans

MAKES 4 SERVINGS

½ cup dried Great Northern beans, soaked 8 hours or overnight

1½ **cups water or chicken broth, divided**

¼ **teaspoon salt, divided**

½ cup uncooked long grain rice

4 ounces fresh green beans, cut into 1-inch pieces (about ¾ cup)

¼ cup prepared pesto

Optional toppings: shredded Parmesan cheese, chopped plum tomatoes and chopped fresh parsley

1. Drain and rinse Great Northern beans. Combine Great Northern beans, 1 cup water and ⅛ teaspoon salt in pot; mix well. Secure lid and move pressure release valve to sealing or locked position. Cook at high pressure 4 minutes.

2. Meanwhile, rinse rice well; drain in fine-mesh strainer. Combine rice, remaining ½ cup water and ⅛ teaspoon salt in small metal bowl that fits inside pot; mix well. Place green beans in center of 12-inch square of foil; sprinkle with additional salt. Bring up two sides of foil over beans; fold foil over several times to create packet. Fold in opposite ends. (Packet should measure about 8×4 inches.)

3. When cooking of Great Northern beans is complete, press Cancel and use quick release. Place rack in pot on top of Great Northern beans; place bowl with rice on rack. Arrange foil packet on top of bowl. (Packet should not entirely cover bowl.) Secure lid and move pressure release valve to sealing or locked position. Cook at high pressure 4 minutes.

4. When cooking is complete, use natural release for 8 minutes, then release remaining pressure. Remove bowl and foil packet from pot. If any liquid remains in bottom of pot with Great Northern beans, press Sauté; cook 1 to 2 minutes or until liquid is evaporated.

5. Add Great Northern beans and green beans to bowl with rice; gently stir in pesto. Serve with desired toppings.

Bulgur Pilaf with Caramelized Onions and Kale

MAKES 4 SERVINGS

1 tablespoon olive oil

1 medium onion, cut into thin wedges

1 clove garlic, minced

2 cups chopped kale

2¾ cups vegetable or chicken broth

1 cup medium grain bulgur

1 teaspoon salt

¼ teaspoon black pepper

1. Press Sauté; heat oil in pot. Add onion; cook about 10 minutes or until golden brown, stirring frequently. Add garlic; cook and stir 1 minute. Add kale; cook and stir about 1 minute or until wilted. Stir in broth, bulgur, salt and pepper; mix well.

2. Secure lid and move pressure release valve to sealing or locked position. Cook at high pressure 8 minutes.

3. When cooking is complete, use natural release for 5 minutes, then release remaining pressure.

Spanish Rice

MAKES 6 TO 8 SERVINGS

2 cups uncooked brown rice

1 tablespoon olive oil

1 small onion, chopped

2 cloves garlic, minced

1 can (about 14 ounces) diced tomatoes with green chiles

1¼ cups chicken broth or water

1 teaspoon salt

1. Rinse rice well; drain in fine-mesh strainer.

2. Press Sauté; heat oil in pot. Add onion and garlic; cook and stir 2 minutes. Add rice; cook and stir 2 minutes. Stir in tomatoes, broth and salt; mix well.

3. Secure lid and move pressure release valve to sealing or locked position. Cook at high pressure 24 minutes.

4. When cooking is complete, use natural release for 10 minutes, then release remaining pressure. Fluff rice with fork.

Easy Cheesy Lasagna

MAKES 4 TO 6 SERVINGS

1 cup ricotta cheese

1¾ cups (5 ounces) shredded Italian blend cheese, divided

1 egg

2½ cups pasta sauce

8 oven-ready (no-boil) lasagna noodles (about 5 ounces)

1½ cups water

1. Spray 7-inch springform pan with nonstick cooking spray. Beat ricotta, ½ cup shredded cheese and egg in small bowl until well blended.

2. Spread ½ cup pasta sauce on bottom of prepared pan. Top with 2 noodles, breaking to fit and cover sauce layer. Spread one third of ricotta mixture over sauce; top with ¼ cup shredded cheese. Repeat layers of sauce, noodles, ricotta mixture and shredded cheese twice, pressing down gently. Top with remaining 2 noodles, ½ cup sauce and ½ cup shredded cheese. Cover pan with foil sprayed with nonstick cooking spray (or use nonstick foil).

3. Pour water into pot. Place rack in pot; place pan on rack using foil sling (see page 8) or handles of rack.

4. Secure lid and move pressure release valve to sealing or locked position. Cook at high pressure 16 minutes. Preheat broiler.

5. When cooking is complete, use natural release for 5 minutes, then release remaining pressure. Uncover lasagna; place pan on baking sheet. Broil about 3 minutes or until top is golden brown in spots. Let stand 5 minutes before serving.

White Beans and Tomatoes

MAKES 8 TO 10 SERVINGS

1 pound dried cannellini beans, soaked 8 hours or overnight

2 **tablespoons olive oil**

2 medium onions, chopped

1 tablespoon minced garlic

1 tablespoon tomato paste

4 **teaspoons dried oregano**

2 **teaspoons salt**

1 can (28 ounces) crushed tomatoes

2 **cups water**

1. Drain and rinse beans. Press Sauté; heat oil in pot. Add onions; cook and stir 5 to 7 minutes or until tender and lightly browned. Add garlic, tomato paste, oregano and salt; cook and stir 1 minute. Stir in beans, tomatoes and water; mix well.

2. Secure lid and move pressure release valve to sealing or locked position. Cook at high pressure 16 minutes.

3. When cooking is complete, use natural release for 10 minutes, then release remaining pressure.

Spinach Risotto

MAKES 4 SERVINGS

2 tablespoons olive oil

2 tablespoons butter, divided

1 shallot, finely chopped

1½ cups uncooked arborio rice

4 cups vegetable broth

1½ teaspoons salt

¼ teaspoon black pepper

2 cups packed baby spinach

½ cup shredded Parmesan cheese

2 tablespoons pine nuts, toasted*

To toast pine nuts, cook in small skillet over medium heat 3 minutes or until lightly browned, stirring frequently.

1. Press Sauté; heat oil and 1 tablespoon butter in pot. Add shallot; cook and stir 2 minutes or until softened. Add rice; cook and stir 3 minutes or until rice is translucent. Stir in broth, salt and pepper; mix well.

2. Secure lid and move pressure release valve to sealing or locked position. Cook at high pressure 6 minutes.

3. When cooking is complete, press Cancel and use quick release.

4. Press Sauté; adjust heat to low. Add spinach to pot; cook about 3 minutes or until spinach is wilted and risotto reaches desired consistency, stirring constantly. Stir in cheese and remaining 1 tablespoon butter until blended. Sprinkle with pine nuts.

Southwestern Mac and Cheese

MAKES 6 TO 8 SERVINGS

3⅓ **cups water**

1 package (16 ounces) uncooked elbow macaroni

1 can (about 14 ounces) diced tomatoes with green peppers and onions

1 **teaspoon salt**

4 cups (16 ounces) shredded Mexican cheese blend, divided

½ cup milk

3 **tablespoons butter**

1 cup salsa

1. Combine water, macaroni, tomatoes and salt in pot; mix well.

2. Secure lid and move pressure release valve to sealing or locked position. Cook at high pressure 4 minutes.

3. When cooking is complete, press Cancel and use quick release.

4. Press Sauté; add 3½ cups cheese, milk and butter to pot. Stir until smooth and well blended. Stir in salsa. Press Cancel. Sprinkle remaining ½ cup cheese over pasta; let stand until melted.

Split Pea Soup

MAKES 4 TO 6 SERVINGS

8 slices bacon, chopped

1 onion, chopped

2 carrots, chopped

1 clove garlic, minced

½ **teaspoon dried thyme**

1 **container (32 ounces) chicken broth**

2 **cups water**

1 package (16 ounces) dried split peas, rinsed and sorted

¾ **teaspoon salt**

½ **teaspoon black pepper**

1 **bay leaf**

1. Press Sauté; cook bacon in pot until crisp. Remove to paper towel-lined plate. Drain off all but 1 tablespoon drippings.

2. Add onion and carrots to pot; cook and stir 5 minutes or until vegetables are softened. Add garlic and thyme; cook and stir 1 minute. Stir in broth and water, scraping up browned bits from bottom of pot. Add split peas, half of bacon, salt, pepper and bay leaf; mix well.

3. Secure lid and move pressure release valve to sealing or locked position. Cook at high pressure 8 minutes.

4. When cooking is complete, use natural release for 10 minutes, then release remaining pressure. Stir soup; remove and discard bay leaf. Top with remaining bacon.

Note:

The soup may seem thin immediately after cooking, but it will thicken upon standing. If prepared in advance and refrigerated, thin the soup with water when reheating until it reaches the desired consistency.

VEGETABLES

Parmesan Potato Wedges
MAKES 4 TO 6 SERVINGS

2 pounds unpeeled red potatoes (about 6 medium), cut into ½-inch wedges

½ cup water

¼ cup finely chopped onion

2 tablespoons butter, cut into small pieces

1¼ teaspoons salt

1 teaspoon dried oregano

¼ teaspoon black pepper

¼ cup grated Parmesan cheese

1. Combine potatoes, water, onion, butter, salt, oregano and pepper in pot; mix well.

2. Secure lid and move pressure release valve to sealing or locked position. Cook at high pressure 3 minutes.

3. When cooking is complete, press Cancel and use quick release.

4. Transfer potatoes to serving platter; sprinkle with cheese.

Coconut Butternut Squash

MAKES 4 TO 6 SERVINGS

1 **tablespoon butter**

½ cup chopped onion

1 butternut squash (about 3 pounds), peeled and cut into 1-inch pieces

1 can (about 13 ounces) coconut milk, well shaken

1 **to 2 tablespoons packed brown sugar, divided**

1¼ **teaspoons salt**

1 **teaspoon pumpkin pie spice**

2 teaspoons grated fresh ginger

2 tablespoons lemon juice

1. Press Sauté; melt butter in pot. Add onion; cook and stir 2 minutes. Add squash, coconut milk, 1 tablespoon brown sugar, salt and pumpkin pie spice; mix well.

2. Secure lid and move pressure release valve to sealing or locked position. Cook at high pressure 6 minutes.

3. When cooking is complete, press Cancel and use quick release.

4. Stir ginger into squash mixture. Use immersion blender to blend squash until smooth. (Or process in food processor or blender.) Stir in lemon juice. Sprinkle individual servings with remaining 1 tablespoon brown sugar, if desired.

Pressure Cooker Collard Greens

MAKES 4 TO 6 SERVINGS

4 slices thick-cut bacon, cut into ½-inch pieces

1 pound collard greens, stems trimmed, roughly chopped

½ **cup water or chicken broth**

1 tablespoon cider vinegar

1 **tablespoon packed brown sugar**

¼ **teaspoon salt**

¼ **teaspoon black pepper**

¼ **teaspoon red pepper flakes**

1. Press Sauté; cook bacon in pot until crisp. Add half of greens; cook 1 minute or until greens begin to wilt, scraping up browned bits from bottom of pot. Stir in remaining greens; cook and stir 1 minute. Add water, vinegar, brown sugar, salt, black pepper and red pepper flakes; mix well.

2. Secure lid and move pressure release valve to sealing or locked position. Cook at high pressure 20 minutes.

3. When cooking is complete, press Cancel and use quick release. Stir greens; serve warm.

Orange-Spiced Glazed Carrots

MAKES 6 SERVINGS

1 package (32 ounces) baby carrots

½ cup orange juice

⅓ **cup packed brown sugar**

3 **tablespoons butter, cut into small pieces**

¾ **teaspoon ground cinnamon**

½ **teaspoon salt**

¼ **teaspoon ground nutmeg**

¼ **cup water**

2 **tablespoons cornstarch**

Grated orange peel and chopped fresh parsley (optional)

1. Combine carrots, orange juice, brown sugar, butter, cinnamon, salt and nutmeg in pot; mix well.

2. Secure lid and move pressure release valve to sealing or locked position. Cook at high pressure 2 minutes.

3. When cooking is complete, press Cancel and use quick release.

4. Stir water into cornstarch in small bowl until smooth. Press Sauté; add cornstarch mixture to pot. Cook and stir 1 to 2 minutes or until sauce thickens. Garnish with orange peel and parsley.

Mashed Root Vegetables

MAKES 6 SERVINGS

1 pound baking potatoes, peeled and cut into 1-inch pieces

1 pound turnips, peeled and cut into 1-inch pieces

12 ounces sweet potatoes, peeled and cut into 1-inch pieces

8 ounces parsnips, peeled and cut into ½-inch pieces

¼ **cup (½ stick) butter, cubed**

⅓ **cup water**

2 **teaspoons salt**

¼ **teaspoon black pepper**

½ cup milk

1. Combine baking potatoes, turnips, sweet potatoes, parsnips, butter, water, salt and pepper in pot; mix well.

2. Secure lid and move pressure release valve to sealing or locked position. Cook at high pressure 10 minutes.

3. When cooking is complete, press Cancel and use quick release.

4. Mash vegetables with potato masher until almost smooth. Press Sauté; stir in milk until blended. Cook and stir about 3 minutes or until milk is absorbed and vegetables reach desired consistency.

Cider Vinaigrette-Glazed Beets

MAKES 6 SERVINGS

6 medium red and/or golden beets (about 3 pounds)

1 cup water

2 tablespoons cider vinegar

1 tablespoon extra virgin olive oil

1 teaspoon Dijon mustard

½ teaspoon packed brown sugar

¾ teaspoon salt

¼ teaspoon black pepper

⅓ cup crumbled blue cheese

1. Cut tops off beets, leaving at least 1 inch of stems. Scrub beets under cold running water with soft vegetable brush, being careful not to break skins. Pour 1 cup water into pot. Place rack in pot; place beets on rack (or use steamer basket to hold beets).

2. Secure lid and move pressure release valve to sealing or locked position. Cook at high pressure 22 minutes.

3. When cooking is complete, use natural release for 10 minutes, then release remaining pressure. Check doneness by inserting paring knife into beets; knife should go in easily. If not, cook an additional 2 to 4 minutes.

4. Whisk vinegar, oil, mustard, brown sugar, salt and pepper in medium bowl until well blended.

5. When beets are cool enough to handle, peel off skins and trim root ends. Cut into wedges. Add warm beets to vinaigrette; toss gently to coat. Sprinkle with cheese. Serve warm or at room temperature.

TIP: The cooking time depends on the size of the beets, which can vary. If beets are not tender enough, secure lid and cook under pressure 2 to 4 minutes longer.

French Onion Soup

MAKES 8 SERVINGS

¼ cup (½ stick) butter

4 medium yellow onions (about 3 pounds), sliced

1 tablespoon sugar

¾ teaspoon salt

¼ teaspoon black pepper

¼ cup dry white wine or sherry

8 cups beef broth

8 to 16 slices French bread

1 cup (4 ounces) shredded Gruyère or Swiss cheese

1. Press Sauté; melt butter in pot. Add onions; cook 15 minutes, stirring occasionally. Add sugar, salt and pepper; cook and stir 5 to 7 minutes or until onions are golden brown. Add wine; cook and stir 1 minute or until evaporated. Stir in broth; mix well.

2. Secure lid and move pressure release valve to sealing or locked position. Cook at high pressure 5 minutes.

3. When cooking is complete, press Cancel and use quick release. Preheat broiler.

4. Ladle soup into individual ovenproof bowls; top with 1 or 2 slices bread and about 2 tablespoons cheese. Place bowls on large baking sheet. Broil 1 to 2 minutes or until bread is toasted and cheese is melted and browned.

Colcannon

MAKES 6 TO 8 SERVINGS

4 slices bacon, chopped

3 pounds russet potatoes, peeled and cut into 1-inch pieces

2 medium leeks, halved lengthwise and thinly sliced

½ **cup water**

1¼ **teaspoons salt**

¼ **teaspoon black pepper**

1 cup milk, divided

2 **tablespoons butter, cut into pieces**

½ small head savoy cabbage (about 1 pound), cored and thinly sliced (about 4 cups)

1. Press Sauté; cook bacon in pot until crisp. Remove to paper towel-lined plate. Add potatoes, leeks, water, salt and pepper to pot; mix well.

2. Secure lid and move pressure release valve to sealing or locked position. Cook at high pressure 5 minutes.

3. When cooking is complete, press Cancel and use quick release.

4. Press Sauté; add ½ cup milk and butter to pot. Cook and stir 1 minute, mashing potatoes until still slightly chunky. Add remaining ½ cup milk and cabbage; cook and stir 2 to 3 minutes or until cabbage is wilted. Stir in bacon.

Brussels Sprouts in Orange Sauce

MAKES 4 SERVINGS

3 oranges

½ **teaspoon salt**

¼ **teaspoon red pepper flakes**

¼ **teaspoon ground cinnamon**

¼ **teaspoon black pepper**

8 ounces fresh brussels sprouts (about 3 cups)

2 **teaspoons cornstarch**

1 teaspoon honey

1. Grate 1 teaspoon peel from oranges. Squeeze ½ cup plus 2 tablespoons juice.

2. Combine ½ cup orange juice, salt, red pepper flakes, cinnamon and black pepper in pot; mix well. Stir in brussels sprouts.

3. Secure lid and move pressure release valve to sealing or locked position. Cook at high pressure 2 minutes.

4. When cooking is complete, press Cancel and use quick release. Remove brussels sprouts to medium bowl with slotted spoon.

5. Stir remaining 2 tablespoons orange juice into cornstarch in small bowl until smooth. Press Sauté; add honey, orange peel and cornstarch mixture to pot. Cook 1 to 2 minutes or until sauce thickens, stirring constantly. Pour sauce over brussels sprouts; stir gently to coat.

Lemon Parmesan Cauliflower

MAKES 6 SERVINGS

1 lemon

1 cup water

3 tablespoons chopped fresh parsley

1 large head cauliflower (2 to 3 pounds), trimmed

1 tablespoon butter

3 cloves garlic, minced

½ teaspoon salt

¼ cup grated Parmesan cheese

1. Grate ½ teaspoon peel from lemon. Squeeze 2 tablespoons juice.

2. Pour water into pot; stir in parsley and lemon peel. Place rack in pot; place cauliflower on rack.

3. Secure lid and move pressure release valve to sealing or locked position. Cook at high pressure 3 minutes.

4. When cooking is complete, press Cancel and use quick release. Remove rack from pot; place cauliflower in large bowl. Reserve ½ cup cooking liquid; discard remaining liquid.

5. Press Sauté; melt butter in pot. Add garlic; cook and stir 1 minute or until fragrant. Add lemon juice, salt and reserved ½ cup cooking liquid; cook and stir until heated through.

6. Spoon lemon sauce over cauliflower; sprinkle with cheese. Cut into wedges to serve.

Spiced Sweet Potatoes

MAKES 4 TO 6 SERVINGS

2½ pounds sweet potatoes, peeled and cut into ½-inch pieces

½ **cup water**

2 **tablespoons packed brown sugar**

1 **teaspoon salt**

1 **teaspoon ground cinnamon**

½ **teaspoon ground nutmeg**

2 **tablespoons butter, cut into small pieces**

½ teaspoon vanilla

1. Combine sweet potatoes, water, brown sugar, salt, cinnamon and nutmeg in pot; mix well.

2. Secure lid and move pressure release valve to sealing or locked position. Cook at high pressure 3 minutes.

3. When cooking is complete, press Cancel and use quick release.

4. Press Sauté; add butter and vanilla to pot. Cook 1 to 2 minutes or until butter is melted, stirring gently to blend.

Balsamic Green Beans with Almonds

MAKES 4 SERVINGS

1 **cup water**

1 pound fresh green beans, trimmed

1 **tablespoon extra virgin olive oil**

2 teaspoons balsamic vinegar

½ **teaspoon salt**

¼ **teaspoon black pepper**

2 tablespoons sliced almonds, toasted*

To toast almonds, cook in small skillet over medium heat 1 to 2 minutes or until lightly browned, stirring frequently.

1. Pour water into pot. Place rack in pot; place beans on rack. (Arrange beans perpendicular to rack to prevent beans from falling through.)

2. Secure lid and move pressure release valve to sealing or locked position. Cook at high pressure 2 minutes.

3. When cooking is complete, press Cancel and use quick release. Remove rack from pot; place beans in large bowl.

4. Add oil, vinegar, salt and pepper; toss to coat. Sprinkle with almonds just before serving.

Garlic Parmesan Spaghetti Squash

MAKES 2 SERVINGS

1 medium spaghetti squash (2 to 2½ pounds)

1 **cup water**

2 **tablespoons extra virgin olive oil**

1 clove garlic, minced

¼ **teaspoon salt**

¼ **teaspoon red pepper flakes**

⅛ **teaspoon black pepper**

½ cup shredded Parmesan cheese

⅓ cup chopped fresh parsley

1. Cut squash in half; remove and discard seeds. Pour water into pot. Place rack in pot; place squash halves cut sides up on rack.

2. Secure lid and move pressure release valve to sealing or locked position. Cook at high pressure 7 minutes.

3. When cooking is complete, press Cancel and use quick release. Remove squash to plate; let stand until cool enough to handle. Use fork to shred squash into long strands, reserving shells for serving, if desired.

4. Pour out cooking water and dry pot. Press Sauté; adjust heat to low. Add oil, garlic, salt, red pepper flakes and black pepper; cook and stir 2 to 3 minutes or until garlic begins to turn golden. Press Cancel. Add squash, cheese and parsley to pot; cook and stir gently just until blended. Serve immediately.

Creamy Tomato Soup

MAKES 6 SERVINGS

2 tablespoons olive oil

2 tablespoons butter

1 large onion, finely chopped

2 cloves garlic, minced

2 teaspoons sugar

1½ teaspoons salt

½ teaspoon dried oregano

2 cans (28 ounces each) peeled Italian plum tomatoes, undrained

½ cup whipping cream

Croutons (optional)

1. Press Sauté; heat oil and butter in pot. Add onion; cook and stir 5 minutes or until softened. Add garlic, sugar, salt and oregano; cook and stir 30 seconds. Stir in tomatoes with juice; mix well.

2. Secure lid and move pressure release valve to sealing or locked position. Cook at high pressure 8 minutes.

3. When cooking is complete, use natural release for 10 minutes, then release remaining pressure.

4. Use hand-held immersion blender to blend soup until smooth. Stir in cream until well blended. Serve soup with croutons, if desired.

TIP: For extra-delicious homemade croutons, cut half of a 9-ounce loaf of focaccia into ½-inch cubes (4 cups); toss with 1 tablespoon olive oil and ½ teaspoon black pepper in a large bowl until coated. Spread on a large baking sheet; bake in a preheated 350°F oven about 10 minutes or until golden brown.

Lemon-Mint Red Potatoes

MAKES 4 SERVINGS

1 lemon

2 pounds new
    red potatoes
    (1½ to 2 inches)

⅓ **cup water**

4 tablespoons
    chopped fresh
    mint, divided

1 **tablespoon olive oil**

1 **teaspoon salt**

¾ **teaspoon Greek
    seasoning or
    dried oregano**

¼ **teaspoon black
    pepper**

1 **tablespoon butter**

1. Grate 1 teaspoon peel from lemon. Squeeze 1 tablespoon juice.

2. Combine potatoes, water, 2 tablespoons mint, oil, salt, lemon peel, Greek seasoning and pepper in pot; mix well.

3. Secure lid and move pressure release valve to sealing or locked position. Cook at high pressure 6 minutes.

4. When cooking is complete, press Cancel and use quick release.

5. Press Sauté; add remaining 2 tablespoons mint, lemon juice and butter to pot. Cook and stir 2 minutes or until butter is melted and potatoes are completely coated.

Beet and Arugula Salad
MAKES 6 TO 8 SERVINGS

1 cup water

8 medium beets (5 to 6 ounces each)

⅓ cup red wine vinegar

¾ teaspoon salt

½ teaspoon black pepper

3 tablespoons extra virgin olive oil

1 package (5 ounces) baby arugula

1 package (4 ounces) goat cheese with garlic and herbs, crumbled

1. Pour water into pot. Place rack in pot; arrange beets on rack (or use steamer basket to hold beets).

2. Secure lid and move pressure release valve to sealing or locked position. Cook at high pressure 20 minutes.

3. When cooking is complete, use natural release for 10 minutes, then release remaining pressure. Set beets aside until cool enough to handle.

4. Meanwhile, whisk vinegar, salt and pepper in large bowl. Slowly add oil in thin steady stream, whisking until well blended. Remove 3 tablespoons dressing to medium bowl.

5. Peel beets and cut into wedges. Add warm beets to large bowl; toss to coat with dressing. Add arugula to medium bowl; toss gently to coat with dressing. Place arugula on platter or plates, top with beets and cheese.

DESERTS

Chocolate Rice Pudding

MAKES 6 SERVINGS

1 **cup water**

1 cup uncooked
   long grain rice

½ **teaspoon salt,**
   divided

1½ cups milk

½ **cup sugar**

2 **tablespoons**
   cornstarch

½ teaspoon vanilla

½ cup semisweet
   chocolate chips

   Whipped cream and
   chocolate curls
   (optional)

1. Combine water, rice and ¼ teaspoon salt in pot; mix well.

2. Secure lid and move pressure release valve to sealing or locked position. Cook at high pressure 4 minutes.

3. When cooking is complete, use natural release for 10 minutes, then release remaining pressure.

4. Whisk milk, sugar, cornstarch, vanilla and remaining ¼ teaspoon salt in medium bowl until well blended. Stir into cooked rice.

5. Press Sauté; cook and stir 5 minutes. Add chocolate chips; stir until melted and smooth. Garnish with whipped cream and chocolate curls.

Superfast Applesauce

MAKES 4 CUPS

2 pounds (about 4 medium) sweet apples (such as Fuji, Gala or Honeycrisp), peeled and cut into 1-inch pieces

2 pounds (about 4 medium) Granny Smith apples, peeled and cut into 1-inch pieces

⅓ **cup water**

2 **to 4 tablespoons packed brown sugar, divided**

1 tablespoon lemon juice

1¼ **teaspoons apple pie spice**

⅛ **teaspoon salt**

1. Combine apples, water, 2 tablespoons brown sugar, lemon juice, apple pie spice and salt in pot; mix well.

2. Secure lid and move pressure release valve to sealing or locked position. Cook at high pressure 4 minutes.

3. When cooking is complete, press Cancel and use quick release.

4. Stir applesauce; taste for seasoning and add remaining 2 tablespoons brown sugar, if desired. If there is excess liquid in pot, press Sauté and cook 2 to 3 minutes or until liquid evaporates. Cool completely before serving.

Peanut Butter Pudding

MAKES 6 SERVINGS

2 cups milk

2 eggs

⅓ cup creamy
   peanut butter

¼ **cup packed
   brown sugar**

¼ teaspoon vanilla

1 **cup water**

   **Shaved chocolate or
   shredded coconut
   (optional)**

1. Spray six 3-ounce ramekins or custard cups with nonstick cooking spray. Combine milk, eggs, peanut butter, brown sugar and vanilla in blender; blend at high speed 1 minute. Pour into prepared ramekins. Cover each ramekin with foil.

2. Pour water into pot; place rack in pot. Arrange ramekins on rack, stacking as necessary.

3. Secure lid and move pressure release valve to sealing or locked position. Cook at high pressure 8 minutes.

4. When cooking is complete, use natural release for 10 minutes, then release remaining pressure.

5. Remove ramekins from pot. Remove foil; cool to room temperature. Refrigerate until chilled. Garnish with shaved chocolate.

Fudgy Double Chocolate Brownies

MAKES 8 SERVINGS

½ cup (1 stick) butter

¾ cup unsweetened cocoa powder

1 cup sugar

2 eggs

⅔ cup all-purpose flour

½ teaspoon salt

½ cup semisweet chocolate chunks or chips

1½ cups water

Vanilla ice cream (optional)

1. Spray 7-inch metal cake pan with nonstick cooking spray.

2. Place butter in medium microwavable bowl; microwave until melted. Stir in cocoa until well blended.

3. Whisk sugar and eggs in large bowl until well blended. Add cocoa mixture; whisk until smooth. Add flour and salt; stir until blended. Stir in chocolate chips. Spread batter in prepared pan; smooth top. Cover with foil.

4. Pour water into pot. Place rack in pot; place pan on rack using foil sling (see page 8) or handles of rack.

5. Secure lid and move pressure release valve to sealing or locked position. Cook at high pressure 25 minutes.

6. When cooking is complete, use natural release for 10 minutes, then release remaining pressure. Uncover; cool on wire rack at least 10 minutes before serving. Serve warm or at room temperature with ice cream, if desired.

Pumpkin Custard

MAKES 6 SERVINGS

3 eggs

1 can (15 ounces) solid-pack pumpkin

1 can (14 ounces) sweetened condensed milk

1 teaspoon ground cinnamon, plus additional for garnish

1 teaspoon finely chopped candied ginger *or* ½ teaspoon ground ginger

¼ teaspoon ground cloves

⅛ teaspoon salt

1 cup water

Whipped cream (optional)

1. Whisk eggs in medium bowl. Add pumpkin, sweetened condensed milk, 1 teaspoon cinnamon, ginger, cloves and salt; whisk until well blended and smooth. Pour into six 6-ounce ramekins or custard cups. Cover each ramekin with foil.

2. Pour water into pot. Place rack in pot; arrange ramekins on rack, stacking as necessary.

3. Secure lid and move pressure release valve to sealing or locked position. Cook at high pressure 8 minutes.

4. When cooking is complete, use natural release.

5. Remove ramekins from pot. Uncover; cool to room temperature. Refrigerate until chilled. Top with whipped cream and additional cinnamon, if desired.

Rich Chocolate Pudding

MAKES 6 SERVINGS

1½ cups whipping
    cream

4 ounces bittersweet
    chocolate,
    chopped

4 egg yolks

⅓ **cup packed
    brown sugar**

1 tablespoon
    unsweetened
    cocoa powder

1 teaspoon vanilla

¼ **teaspoon salt**

1¼ **cups water**

1. Heat cream to a simmer in medium saucepan over medium heat. Remove from heat. Add chocolate; stir until chocolate is melted and mixture is smooth.

2. Whisk egg yolks, brown sugar, cocoa, vanilla and salt in large bowl until well blended. Gradually add warm chocolate mixture, whisking constantly until blended. Strain into 6- to 7-inch (1½-quart) soufflé dish. Cover with foil.

3. Pour water into pot. Place rack in pot; place soufflé dish on rack using foil sling (see page 8) or handles of rack.

4. Secure lid and move pressure release valve to sealing or locked position. Cook at low pressure 22 minutes.

5. When cooking is complete, use natural release for 5 minutes, then release remaining pressure.

6. Remove soufflé dish from pot. Uncover; cool to room temperature. Cover and refrigerate at least 3 hours or up to 2 days.

Plum Bread Pudding

MAKES 6 SERVINGS

6 cups cubed brioche, egg bread or challah (1-inch cubes)

1½ tablespoons butter

2 large plums, pitted and cut into thin wedges

⅓ cup plus ½ tablespoon sugar, divided

3 eggs

¾ cup half-and-half

½ cup milk

¼ teaspoon salt

¼ teaspoon ground cinnamon

1¼ cups water

Whipping cream or vanilla ice cream (optional)

1. Preheat oven to 400°F. Spray 6- to 7-inch (1½-quart) soufflé dish with nonstick cooking spray.

2. Spread bread cubes in single layer on ungreased baking sheet. Bake 6 to 7 minutes or until lightly toasted, stirring halfway through baking time.

3. Meanwhile, melt butter in large skillet over medium-high heat. Add plums and ½ tablespoon sugar; cook 2 minutes or until plums are softened and release juices. Beat eggs in large bowl. Add half-and-half, milk, remaining ⅓ cup sugar, salt and cinnamon; mix well. Add plums and toasted bread cubes; stir gently to coat. Pour into prepared soufflé dish. Cover with foil.

4. Pour water into pot. Place rack in pot; place soufflé dish on rack using foil sling (see page 8) or handles of rack.

5. Secure lid and move pressure release valve to sealing or locked position. Cook at high pressure 35 minutes. When cooking is complete, use natural release for 10 minutes, then release remaining pressure.

6. Remove soufflé dish from pot. Let stand, covered, 15 minutes. Remove foil; serve warm with cream, if desired.

Chocolate Truffle Cake

MAKES 8 SERVINGS

Unsweetened
  cocoa powder

12 ounces bittersweet
  (60%) chocolate,
  chopped

½ **cup (1 stick) butter,
  cut into pieces**

5 eggs, separated

1 teaspoon vanilla

¼ **teaspoon salt**

½ **cup granulated sugar**

1½ **cups water**

Powdered sugar and
  fresh raspberies
  (optional)

1. Spray 7-inch springform pan with nonstick cooking spray; dust with cocoa powder.

2. Combine chocolate and butter in large microwavable bowl; microwave on MEDIUM (50%) 2 minutes or until melted and smooth, stirring after each minute. Set aside to cool 5 minutes. Beat in egg yolks and vanilla until well blended.

3. Beat egg whites and salt in medium bowl with electric mixer at medium speed until frothy. Gradually add granulated sugar, beating at medium-high speed until almost firm (but not stiff) peaks form. Fold one third of egg whites into chocolate mixture until blended. Gently fold in remaining egg whites just until blended. Spread batter in prepared pan; smooth top.

4. Pour water into pot. Place rack in pot; place pan on rack using foil sling (see page 8) or handles of rack.

5. Secure lid and move pressure release valve to sealing or locked position. Cook at high pressure 15 minutes.

6. When cooking is complete, use natural release for 10 minutes, then release remaining pressure. Cool in pan on wire rack 30 minutes; refrigerate at least 2 hours before serving. Remove side of pan; garnish with powdered sugar and raspberries.

Applesauce Custard

MAKES 6 SERVINGS

1½ cups unsweetened applesauce

½ **teaspoon ground cinnamon**

¼ **teaspoon salt**

4 eggs, at room temperature

½ cup half-and-half

¼ cup unsweetened apple juice concentrate

⅛ **teaspoon ground nutmeg**

1¼ **cups water**

1. Combine applesauce, cinnamon and salt in medium bowl; mix well. Whisk in eggs, half-and-half and apple juice concentrate until well blended. Pour into 6- to 7-inch (1½-quart) soufflé dish; sprinkle with nutmeg. Cover with foil.

2. Pour water into pot. Place rack in pot; place soufflé dish on rack using foil sling (see page 8) or handles of rack.

3. Secure lid and move pressure release valve to sealing or locked position. Cook at high pressure 30 minutes.

4. When cooking is complete, use natural release for 10 minutes, then release remaining pressure.

5. Remove soufflé dish from pot. Uncover; cool to room temperature. Serve at room temperature or chilled.

Chocolate Surprise Crème Brûlée

MAKES 5 SERVINGS

3 ounces bittersweet chocolate, finely chopped

5 egg yolks

1¾ cups whipping cream

¾ **cup granulated sugar, divided**

¼ **teaspoon salt**

1 teaspoon vanilla

1 **cup water**

1. Spray bottoms of five 6-ounce ramekins or custard cups with nonstick cooking spray. Divide chocolate evenly among ramekins.

2. Whisk egg yolks in medium bowl. Combine cream, ½ cup sugar and salt in medium saucepan; bring to a simmer over medium heat. Slowly pour ¼ cup hot cream mixture into egg yolks, whisking until blended. Add remaining cream mixture in thin steady stream, whisking constantly. Pour through fine-mesh strainer into clean bowl. Stir in vanilla. Ladle custard mixture into prepared ramekins over chocolate. Cover each ramekin with foil.

3. Pour water into pot. Place rack in pot; arrange ramekins on rack, stacking as necessary.

4. Secure lid and move pressure release valve to sealing or locked position. Cook at high pressure 6 minutes.

5. When cooking is complete, use natural release for 10 minutes, then release remaining pressure. Remove ramekins from pot. Uncover; cool to room temperature. Refrigerate until ready to serve.

6. Just before serving, preheat broiler. Place ramekins on baking sheet; sprinkle tops of custards with remaining ¼ cup sugar. Broil 4 inches from heat 1 to 2 minutes or until sugar bubbles and browns.

Pumpkin Bread Pudding

MAKES 4 SERVINGS

1 cup whole milk

2 eggs

½ cup canned pumpkin

⅓ **cup packed brown sugar**

1½ **teaspoons ground cinnamon**

1 teaspoon vanilla

¼ **teaspoon salt**

¼ **teaspoon ground nutmeg**

8 slices cinnamon raisin bread, torn into small pieces (about 4 cups)

1¼ **cups water**

Prepared caramel sauce or ice cream topping (optional)

1. Spray 6- to 7-inch (1½-quart) soufflé dish with nonstick cooking spray. Whisk milk, eggs, pumpkin, brown sugar, cinnamon, vanilla, salt and nutmeg in large bowl until well blended. Add bread cubes; toss to coat. Pour into prepared soufflé dish; cover with foil.

2. Pour water into pot. Place rack in pot; place soufflé dish on rack using foil sling (see page 8) or handles of rack.

3. Secure lid and move pressure release valve to sealing or locked position. Cook at high pressure 40 minutes.

4. When cooking is complete, use natural release for 10 minutes, then release remaining pressure.

5. Remove soufflé dish from pot. Uncover; cool 15 minutes. Serve warm with caramel sauce, if desired.

Southern Sweet Potato Custard

MAKES 4 SERVINGS

1 can (16 ounces) cut sweet potatoes, drained

1 can (12 ounces) evaporated milk, divided

½ **cup packed brown sugar**

2 eggs, lightly beaten

1 **teaspoon ground cinnamon**

½ **teaspoon ground ginger**

¼ **teaspoon salt**

1¼ **cups water**

Whipped cream and ground nutmeg (optional)

1. Combine sweet potatoes and ¼ cup evaporated milk in food processor or blender; process until smooth. Add remaining milk, brown sugar, eggs, cinnamon, ginger and salt; process until well blended. Pour into 6- to 7-inch (1½-quart) soufflé dish. Cover with foil.

2. Pour water into pot. Place rack in pot; place soufflé dish on rack using foil sling (see page 8) or handles of rack.

3. Secure lid and move pressure release valve to sealing or locked position. Cook at high pressure 40 minutes.

4. When cooking is complete, use natural release for 10 minutes, then release remaining pressure.

5. Remove soufflé dish from pot. Uncover; cool 30 minutes. Garnish with whipped cream and nutmeg.

Pressure Cooking Times

Meat	Minutes under Pressure	Pressure	Release
Beef, Bone-in Short Ribs	35 to 45	High	Natural
Beef, Brisket	60 to 75	High	Natural
Beef, Ground	8	High	Natural
Beef, Roast (round, rump or shoulder)	60 to 70	High	Natural
Beef, Stew Meat	20 to 25	High	Natural or Quick
Lamb, Chops	5 to 10	High	Quick
Lamb, Leg or Shanks	35 to 40	High	Natural
Lamb, Stew Meat	12 to 15	High	Quick
Pork, Baby Back Ribs	25 to 30	High	Natural
Pork, Chops	7 to 10	High	Quick
Pork, Ground	5	High	Quick
Pork, Loin	15 to 25	High	Natural
Pork, Shoulder or Butt	45 to 60	High	Natural
Pork, Stew Meat	15 to 20	High	Quick

Poultry

	Minutes under Pressure	Pressure	Release
Chicken Breasts, Bone-in	7 to 10	High	Quick
Chicken Breasts, Boneless	5 to 8	High	Quick
Chicken Thigh, Bone-in	10 to 14	High	Natural
Chicken Thigh, Boneless	8 to 10	High	Natural
Chicken Wings	10 to 12	High	Quick
Chicken, Whole	22 to 26	High	Natural
Eggs, Hard-Cooked (3 to 12)	9	Low	Quick
Turkey Breast, Bone-in	25 to 30	High	Natural
Turkey Breast, Boneless	15 to 20	High	Natural
Turkey Legs	35 to 40	High	Natural
Turkey, Ground	8 to 10	High	Quick

Seafood

	Minutes under Pressure	Pressure	Release
Cod	2 to 3	Low	Quick
Crab	2 to 3	Low	Quick
Halibut	6	Low	Quick
Mussels	1 to 2	Low	Quick
Salmon	4 to 5	Low	Quick
Scallops	1	Low	Quick
Shrimp	2 to 3	Low	Quick
Swordfish	4 to 5	Low	Quick
Tilapia	3	Low	Quick

Dried Beans and Legumes

	Unsoaked	Soaked	Pressure	Release
Black Beans	22 to 25	8 to 10	High	Natural
Black-Eyed Peas	9 to 11	3 to 5	High	Natural
Cannellini Beans	30 to 35	8 to 10	High	Natural
Chickpeas	35 to 40	18 to 22	High	Natural
Great Northern Beans	25 to 30	7 to 10	High	Natural
Kidney Beans	20 to 25	8 to 12	High	Natural
Lentils, Brown or Green	10 to 12	n/a	High	Natural
Lentils, Red or Yellow Split	1	n/a	High	Natural
Navy Beans	20 to 25	7 to 8	High	Natural
Pinto Beans	22 to 25	8 to 10	High	Natural
Split Peas	8 to 10	n/a	High	Natural

Grains

	Liquid per Cup	Minutes under Pressure	Pressure	Release
Barley, Pearl	2	18 to 22	High	Natural
Barley, Whole	2½	30 to 35	High	Natural
Bulgur	3	8	High	Natural
Farro	2	10 to 12	High	Natural
Grits, Medium	4	12 to 15	High	10 minute natural
Millet	1½	1	High	Natural
Oats, Rolled	2	4 to 5	High	10 minute natural
Oats, Steel-Cut	3	10 to 13	High	10 minute natural
Quinoa	1½	1	High	10 minute natural
Polenta, Instant	3	5	High	5 minute natural
Rice, Arborio	2	6 to 7	High	Quick
Rice, Brown	1	22	High	10 minute natural
Rice, White Long Grain	1	4	High	10 minute natural

Vegetables	Minutes under Pressure	Pressure	Release
Artichokes, Whole	9 to 12	High	Natural
Beets, Medium Whole	18 to 24	High	Quick
Brussels Sprouts, Whole	2 to 3	High	Quick
Cabbage, Sliced	3 to 5	High	Quick
Carrots, Sliced	2 to 4	High	Quick
Cauliflower, Florets	2 to 3	High	Quick
Cauliflower, Whole	3 to 5	High	Quick
Corn on the Cob	2 to 4	High	Quick
Eggplant	3 to 4	High	Quick
Fennel, Sliced	3 to 4	High	Quick
Green Beans	2 to 4	High	Quick
Kale	3	High	Quick
Leeks	3	High	Quick
Okra	3	High	Quick
Potatoes, Baby or Fingerling	6 to 10	High	Natural
Potatoes, New	7 to 9	High	Natural
Potatoes, 1-inch pieces	4 to 6	High	Quick
Potatoes, Sweet, 1-inch pieces	3	High	Quick
Potatoes, Sweet, Whole	8 to 12	High	Natural
Spinach	1	High	Quick
Squash, Acorn, Halved	7	High	Natural
Squash, Butternut, 1-inch pieces	4 to 6	High	Quick
Squash, Spaghetti, Halved	6 to 10	High	Natural
Tomatoes, cut into pieces for sauce	5	High	Natural

Index

Metric Conversion Chart

VOLUME MEASUREMENTS (dry)

1/8 teaspoon = 0.5 mL
1/4 teaspoon = 1 mL
1/2 teaspoon = 2 mL
3/4 teaspoon = 4 mL
1 teaspoon = 5 mL
1 tablespoon = 15 mL
2 tablespoons = 30 mL
1/4 cup = 60 mL
1/3 cup = 75 mL
1/2 cup = 125 mL
2/3 cup = 150 mL
3/4 cup = 175 mL
1 cup = 250 mL
2 cups = 1 pint = 500 mL
3 cups = 750 mL
4 cups = 1 quart = 1 L

VOLUME MEASUREMENTS (fluid)

1 fluid ounce (2 tablespoons) = 30 mL
4 fluid ounces (1/2 cup) = 125 mL
8 fluid ounces (1 cup) = 250 mL
12 fluid ounces (1 1/2 cups) = 375 mL
16 fluid ounces (2 cups) = 500 mL

WEIGHTS (mass)

1/2 ounce = 15 g
1 ounce = 30 g
3 ounces = 90 g
4 ounces = 120 g
8 ounces = 225 g
10 ounces = 285 g
12 ounces = 360 g
16 ounces = 1 pound = 450 g

DIMENSIONS

1/16 inch = 2 mm
1/8 inch = 3 mm
1/4 inch = 6 mm
1/2 inch = 1.5 cm
3/4 inch = 2 cm
1 inch = 2.5 cm

OVEN TEMPERATURES

250°F = 120°C
275°F = 140°C
300°F = 150°C
325°F = 160°C
350°F = 180°C
375°F = 190°C
400°F = 200°C
425°F = 220°C
450°F = 230°C

BAKING PAN SIZES

Utensil	Size in Inches/Quarts	Metric Volume	Size in Centimeters
Baking or Cake Pan (square or rectangular)	8×8×2	2 L	20×20×5
	9×9×2	2.5 L	23×23×5
	12×8×2	3 L	30×20×5
	13×9×2	3.5 L	33×23×5
Loaf Pan	8×4×3	1.5 L	20×10×7
	9×5×3	2 L	23×13×7
Round Layer Cake Pan	8×1½	1.2 L	20×4
	9×1½	1.5 L	23×4
Pie Plate	8×1¼	750 mL	20×3
	9×1¼	1 L	23×3
Baking Dish or Casserole	1 quart	1 L	—
	1½ quart	1.5 L	—
	2 quart	2 L	—